TONY McMANUS

THE RADICAL FIELD

Kenneth White and Geopoetics

THE HIGHLINER SERIES

Sandstone Press Ltd
Highland, Scotland

THE HIGHLINER SERIES

THE RADICAL FIELD

First published 2007 in Great Britain by Sandstone Press Ltd
PO Box 5725, One High Street, Dingwall, Ross-shire, IV15 9WJ

ISBN: 978-1-905207-14-5

Designed and typeset in Dutch
by River Design, Edinburgh.
Printed and bound in the European Union.

Scottish **Arts** Council

The publisher acknowledges subsidy from the Scottish Arts Council.

SANDSTONE PRESS
CONTEMPORARY QUALITY READING

www.sandstonepress.com

CONTENTS

Foreword   vii

PART ONE: THE INITIAL GROUND   1
1. Family Alchemy   2
2. Shore and Moor   7
3. The Glasgow Student   15
4. Munich: Isolation and Meditation   22
5. Paris: The Incandescent Zone   25
6. Gourgounel: Resourcing   31
7. First Publications   36
8. On the British Literary Scene   41
9. The Departure   47
Notes   52

PART TWO: THE EMERGENT FIELD   59
1. A Scottish Constellation   60
2. Universal Ancestor: The Shaman   68
3. Cultural Analysis Now   79
4. The Drifting Dawn   87
5. Radical European Thought   95
6. On American Trails   104
7. Investigations into Asia   108
8. Pathways in Science   118
9. From Scotland to Alba and Beyond   133
Notes   149

PART THREE: OPEN WORLD WRITING   159

1. The Essay   160

2. The Waybook   165

3. The Poem of the Earth   179

Notes   197

Bibliographies   201

FOREWORD

If I set out to write this book on the work of Kenneth White and geopoetics, it's because it has been obvious to me for some time now, not only that White stands among the most significant writers and thinkers working today, but that his work belongs to a very rare category, one that stands outside those currently in vogue.

This has already been recognised in contexts other than the English language one.

Looking through the already bulky archives gathering around White's work in the National Library of Scotland in Edinburgh and the Fonds Kenneth White in the city of Bordeaux, one comes across statements such as these: 'White's polymorphous work is out to de-compartmentalize thought and create new cultural space' (*L'Hebdo*, Geneva); 'Kenneth White lifts the mind from so much stale discourse and raises intelligence to a rare level' (*Le Figaro littéraire*, Paris); 'At a time when a certain mediocrity is reaching planetary proportions, one of us has stood up, turned his back and, possessed of real knowledge, moved off' (*Revue des Belles-Lettres*, Geneva); 'White belongs to a silent vanguard, in solitary rebellion against not only the entrenched establishments, but the modernist cliques' (*Review of the University of Mexico*); 'Travelling out on his own ways, Kenneth

White is bound to appear more and more as the foremost English poet of these times' (*Le Nouvel Observateur*, Paris).

All this may come as a surprise to some who, even now, some years after his reconnection with the British scene and the ongoing publication of his work in English, have heard very little of Kenneth White. But this is no new thing in cultural history.

In order to go far, Kenneth White moved out and away.

Born and educated in Scotland, continuing his studies in Germany and France, White started publishing from London, but very soon, looking for the space in which to develop the necessary work, he made for France. Over the following years, his books would be published, in French, from Paris, then translated from the French into other languages, while the English manuscripts remained in manuscript, simply because, deep down, White felt the cultural context in Britain and other English language countries wasn't ready, and he was in no hurry.

Contact with this 'intellectual nomad' was re-established in 1989, when his books began to appear in English, this time from Edinburgh. It had been in fact White's intention, when the time seemed opportune for him to renew his relationship with the English language scene, to do so from Scotland. There were several reasons for that. One was that he felt he was continuing a deep Scottish movement and wanted to underline that continuity. Then, he saw the British centre as marked by a combination of conservative tradition and triviality, and he wanted to try and open up another space, from what had long been considered as 'the periphery'. A third factor on his mind was the idea of renewing Scotland politically and culturally within the context of the new Europe.

It is the aim of the present study, based for its documentation on a long analysis of White's work both in English and in French, as well as in conversations with him over the years, to lay out the main lines of White's long journey into geopoetics.

Tony McManus
Edinburgh, September 2001

PART ONE:
THE INITIAL GROUND

*I was born on that Atlantic shore of Europe and
I have its topography imprinted on my mind.*

KENNETH WHITE,
On Scottish Ground

1. Family Alchemy

Kenneth White was born in the Gorbals area of Glasgow on 28 April 1936. His father was a railway signalman and an avid reader of literature and political works in an era when self-motivated study was a characteristic of the Scottish working class through institutions such as the Left Book Club and through charismatic individuals such as John MacLean, the Marxist and republican, whose classes in economics and politics in Glasgow during the first decades of the century attracted thousands of students from the industrial communities.

In his early writings, Kenneth White explores his 'family alchemy' in some detail. In an autobiographical essay entitled 'Hell's Blazes'[1], he writes of his grandfather, Jock White, who played the bagpipes in travelling shows and was something of a character – 'of the devil's camp from first to last' – and of his Highland wife, the poet's grandmother, a Mackenzie, in whose house they ate 'blackish-red venison sent down from Inverness'.

White makes few references to his mother in his work, but in an unusual (for him) piece, included in an anthology of authors writing about their mothers[2], he says this:

> Perhaps a mother is like the concentration of a culture.
> I believe mine was a personification of the conflicts, the contradictions, the problems of Scottish culture.

She was a 'secretive' woman in whom White thinks 'lurked a lot of violence'. Her father, 'an intelligent man', was a foundry worker who took himself off to the USA one day, leaving his family behind, and came back later only to give himself over to the drink. Enough of Glasgow's black humour remains with White for him to recall one day when this 'secretive, silent' woman came after him with an axe:

> I found refuge in the toilet. She smashed through the door with the axe. I don't think she would have planted it in my skull, though. Maybe my shoulder?

He remembers the 'blue water of boiling soap' in the steamie, the 'miracle' of cake-making in which all the various ingredients 'finally cohere', and how 'from a thread of wool you could arrive at something which held together' using a technique which could be explained in four words: 'in, over, through, off. That's like a summary of life!' But what comes across strongest, as well as affection, is a heartfelt regret for a life that was self-denied:

> What desires she had had she never spoke of them to me. She fell in love with my father. She became mother of a family, and she turned inwards . . .

His abiding memory of her is powerfully poetic: 'This woman, silent, her gaze plunged in to the fire.'

His mother was a Cameron of Glasgow. As to the Whites of Glasgow and Edinburgh, Jock White postulated an original MacGregor patronymic which would have been banned during the proscription periods that this clan, even more rebellious and marginalised than the Camerons, suffered, which led to the adoption of physical description – fair, black, red, white – as surname. William White seems to have been a very different character from his wife:

> I often saw her cry, even explode sometimes [. . .] in contrast with my father who never allowed himself to be beaten, who struggled, who talked of changing society . . .

His mother hoped, like all working-class parents of that time, that her son would graduate into the middle classes, become a doctor or a lawyer. When the subject arose, White would say that he wanted to be 'a beachcomber' and he recalls that 'my father would laugh and say I was going to end up as "an intellectual tramp"'. Another version of this paternal quip was 'one of these days you'll go off and do a Gauguin'.

These are not the only uncannily prescient contributions his father made to White's future. When the writer was three years old, his father took the family off to live in Fairlie, a little village on the west coast just south of Largs because he wished his children to grow up with access to the natural world.

William White worked in the railway signalman's box on the line at the north end of the village. White has interesting things to say of the work his father was responsible for in that cabin, which impressed him with its levers, flags and registers. The image of this signalbox crops up intermittently in White's work. In *Pilgrim of the Void*, on a train to Sheung Shui, he recalls the signalbox slate his father had given him to write upon – 'In some sense my writing began in a signalbox.'³ In several texts we come across images such as this from 'Trans-Europe Express'⁴:

A signal cabin flashes by
I hear my father
whistling in the silence

White talks about 'three groups of signs'[5] in the village. The first group consisted of the snatches of conversation, that is normal social discourse, he heard here and there and collected as a youngster. He wrote them down and, dissatisfied with their random aimlessness, tried to give them some coherence.

In the signalbox was a contrasting 'second group' of signs, a world where exact communication was the difference between life and death:

a context of pure semiology

a place of precise codes
scrupulously respected

The 'third group of signs' was to be found in the landscape surrounding Fairlie. I shall return to these later.

It may seem strange to begin a book on Kenneth White, whose work is all about breaking free from the socio-personal context, with these social and familial details. But it is important to have some idea of the particular context from which he moved away because he did so not out of enmity, nor in the 'drop-out' mode of the fifties and sixties, but out of an intellectual awareness which owes something to that background.

Talking of his childhood reading, he identifies tastes and tendencies which indicate his future itinerary:

> Around the age of fifteen, my favourite book was George Borrow's Lavengro [...] which is the account of the trials and peregrinations of a wandering scholar, in particular with a tribe of gypsies. It may not come as a surprise that my favourite poem around the same time was Matthew Arnold's 'The Scholar Gypsy'. A good few years later, I still have pleasure in reading these texts. Who knows if the notion of 'intellectual nomadism', which was to occupy me so long theoretically at one point and which has been a practice of my life, didn't have its germ, or at least one of its germs, in that tale and in that poem.[6]

Grenfell's *The Romance of Labrador* and Hugo's *The Toilers of the Sea* are other significant texts from his childhood. Among Scottish writers, Stevenson was favoured over Scott for the 'vagrancy' as well as for the 'rhythm' of his writing. The young White was also engaged in local studies of the history, geology and archaeology of Ayrshire, which then extended into similar studies of Scotland. His first public piece of writing was an essay, written at the age of sixteen, on the archaeology of Ayrshire, which was lodged in the public library in Ayr. Interestingly, he indicates that 'what counted lastingly was the work leading up to (the essay) and the "lines" I got from the books I read'[7]. Among these were Donald Mackenzie's *Scotland, the Ancient Kingdom*, Simpson's *The Celtic Church in Scotland*, Irving's *Lives of the Poets* – all of these works indicating further 'lines' to pursue: Ninian and the *candida casa* at Whithorn, Duns Scotus, George Buchanan, Thomas Urquhart...

As we proceed into the life and work of Kenneth White we will see that the themes and images which are evoked by this west of Scotland childhood inform a work which has reached out to cover the globe, especially the cultural globe. Even White himself seems occasionally surprised by the range and distance his work has covered from what some would consider inauspicious roots:

FAMILY ALCHEMY

When I think of them all

a dancing rascal
a red-bearded fisherman
a red-flag waver
a red-eyed scholar
a drunken motherfucker . . .

I take a look in the mirror
and I wonder[8]

2. Shore and Moor

It is in his removal of the family to the coast that White senior most influenced the future of his son, for so much of what Kenneth White has come to do has its origins in that landscape and seascape. In his long poem, 'Walking the Coast', he writes of the sound of the sea (quoting in the by-going, both for sound and sense, an old Welsh poem) which was a constant feature of his surroundings:

in that house of three storeys
only yards from the sea
  a house with
        anwar don lavar
levawr wrthi
a wild wave talking
  and clashing beside it[9]

He recalls[10] the time spent on the shore gathering wrack, picking shellfish for the London market, building huts, 'collecting birds' eggs, shells and stones from the shore', imitating the cries of seals and those gulls which were to become of almost totemic significance in his writing. In a lecture given at the University of Tübingen[11], White described the significance of shore:

> I take 'seaboard' (littoral, shore) to be particularly significant space. We are close there to the beginnings of life, we cannot but be aware there of primordial rhythms (tidal, meteorological). In that space, too, we have one foot, as it were, in humanity (inhabited, inscribed space) the other in the non-human cosmos (chaos-cosmos, chaosmos) – and I think it is vitally important to keep that dialogue alive. It may be for reasons similar to those I have just evoked that in a text belonging to a tradition which I perhaps bear in my bones, an old Celtic text, 'The Talk of the Two Scholars' (*Imacallam in da thuarad*), we read: 'the shore was always a place of predilection for the poets'.

White taps into this particular relationship with the sea that permeates Celtic literature and thought when, in the long poem, 'Scotia Deserta'[12], he recalls the stained-glass window in the Fairlie Kirk which shows St. Kentigern on the seashore, book in hand, gulls careering about him and he preaching to them:

> *I'd be gazing at the window*
> *and forgetting the sermon*
> *(all about good and evil*
> *with a lot of mangled metaphor*
> *and heavy comparison)*
> *eager to get back out*
> *onto the naked shore*
> *there to walk for hours on end*
> *with a book sometimes in my hand*
> *but never a thought of preaching in my mind*
>
> *trying to grasp at something*
> *that wanted no godly name*
> *something that took the form*
> *of blue waves and grey rock*
> *and that tasted of salt*

It was, in many ways, a vision of his own future and White's writings constantly return, directly or implicitly, to that vision and its component images of the hermit-monk, the light, gulls, things existing not in society, but 'out there', on the 'naked shore' with the crucial difference that there is no idealism ('no godly name') spurring him on but a desire for direct contact with the reality of the world and a form of expression for that contact which would be as real and natural as that world, taking the form of 'blue waves and grey rock'.

These lines are written in adulthood, of course, and give retrospective understanding and shape to the boy's behaviour. Nevertheless, it is important to underline how radical a vision this was for a youngster in 1940s' Scotland where the power of established biblical religion (all those 'mangled metaphors' about 'good and evil') was all pervasive:

> As a child, thanks to a Scottish religious education, I was up to my neck in the Bible. You will understand me if I say that as soon as I began to 'see clearly', I much preferred 'the sound of waves in the morning on the white pebbled beaches' to biblical passages such as this (Revelations 19: 12–16), 'His eyes? A burning flame. On his head, several crowns [. . .] the coat which covers him is soaked with blood. And his name? The Word of God.' There we're in a real nightmare. And we've been in it for too long.[13]

Again, White is contrasting the naturalist tradition deriving from the Finnian literature surrounding the figure of Fionn MacCumhail, which so influenced the peculiar Christianity of these islands as represented by figures such as Kentigern, with the 'nightmare' anthropomorphism of the Judaeo-Roman culture which was embraced by the established church.

I shall come back to this intellectual strand on the shore of White's childhood experience later. First it is necessary to explore another 'place of predilection' in White's childhood, where he found 'the third group of signs' referred to earlier, a place of which he writes:

> there lay the beginnings
> of my cosmopoetic ramblings[14]

This is the 'territory' accessed via the Craigie Rock at the north end of the village of Fairlie and which takes you up through farms and a beechwood onto the moors which ascend towards the hill sitting between the Fairlie coast and the Clyde valley, the Kaim. From there you can sense that this corner of Ayrshire is like a microcosm of Scotland. Out there behind you is the Atlantic Ocean with its islands, notably Arran, its mountains as constant a presence in Fairlie as is the sound of the sea; the village with its kirk, its war memorial and its railway line; the fertile farmland and green grazing grounds; the beeches and sycamores giving way to birches; the land of rock and moor, bleak and exposed, purpling with heather as it climbs to the bare rounded crest of the Kaim. Sea, islands, settlements, woods, moors and hills, the cold and the wind and the rain, the gulls, the crows and the herons – this is the area White refers to as 'up the back' and which, from the age of eleven he began to frequent constantly:

> After a period of belonging to gangs, which was my introduction to politics, I was then entering a long period of isolation, and I was up to all kinds of solitary practices, all of which were connected with the territory.[15]

He engaged there in what he calls a 'meditative wandering' and talks of 'the gulls circling and caterwauling around the cowp' and 'a band of heron – in spring the ground would be strewn with broken pale-blue shells, blood-smeared, smelling of the sea'. He explains how, there, 'something more archaic, more radical [. . .] manifested itself' in him as he acquired 'a collection of little skeletons of birds and animals'[16]. He relates this directly to his writing: 'If my writing has any concrete beauty, it is probably because of these things.' Characteristically, he sees his activities in a wider human and historical perspective. As he writes in that first book:

> The Scot is a nomad, like the Scythian, his ancestor. But
> there is in him also a quietude. It is this twofold delight in
> movement and tranquility which I feel on the moors.
> Perhaps, originally, the area of wandering was the great
> Eurasian steppe which extends from China to the Danube;
> but a moor on the west of Scotland is enough. Space to
> move in and tranquility to see in. That is the original ground
> of poetry.

These experiences and that conclusion about the 'ground of
poetry' crop up time and again in White's work. One early
poem[17] sums up the area and its effect on him, but is also of
particular interest because it has a great deal to say about
explaining the nature of the experience and its wider cultural
relevance and also about the nature and form of the expression
which the writer feels is a necessary result of the experience:

> *MORNING WALK*
>
> *It was a cold slow-moving mist*
> *clotted round the sun, clinging*
> *to the small white sun, and the earth*
> *was alone and lonely, and a great bird*
> *harshly squawked from the heronry*
> *as the boy walked under the beeches*
> *seeing the broken pale-blue shells*
> *and the moist piles of mouldering leaves.*

Here the word 'seeing' has a peculiar force: this is a poem
about perception. One might have expected 'looking' – what

'seeing' does is to heighten and deepen the perceptual experience the boy is having: the unspoken last line is 'as if for the first time'. The word's force is strengthened by its use in participial form just after two active verbs, 'squawked' and 'walked', whose rhyme helps transmit their active nature into the participial form of 'seeing'. This causes the reader to understand that this 'seeing' is not something that is happening *to* the boy, he is *doing* it. This form also allows the word to act as a noun and a verb at the same time, that is, to make the abstract and the concrete co-exist: *this* boy seeing *those* pale-blue shells, but also the *idea* of 'seeing pale-blue shells'. This, plus the expression of colour, 'pale-blue' (the repetition of the 'l' sound unites the three words 'pale-blue shells' into a strongly visual expression) also leads us, the reader, to 'see' them too. And that last line is an image of the true focus of our perception: the *earth* in a sensual, erotic expression: 'moist, mouldering leaves'.

This is an early poem and it has obvious signs of conscious crafting. But there is in addition the sense of a language which is the natural spontaneous expression of perception of the realities of the world, a language which seeks to *reveal* that world, is clearly already present in this young writer's mind in contrast to the type of poetry we are most used to which, through its elaboration of metaphor, metre and word-play, succeeds more in revealing the poet than the experience which is the supposed subject-matter of the poem.

Here we are at the heart of White's poetics and I shall come back to these matters more fully later. First, though, why does White apparently turn aside from the human world, the socio-personal concerns which are the focus of modernity and the meat and drink of its artists? What is this poetics which often

13

seems to step outside the norm in its apparent disregard for formal techniques? I use the words 'apparently' and 'seems' deliberately as White clearly does not see his work as being unhuman or informal, nor, for that matter, do I. Quite the contrary in fact, and I shall develop these points later. But first we must return to the biographical account and study White's evolving negativism towards the socio-personal context.

It is important to establish first of all that White played his role in the social context which was his village and the town of Largs where he attended secondary school. We have already noted his reference to 'gangs', and that he played the child's part in the local economy (a necessary contribution to family finances in those days, not the gateway to personal consumerism which it has now become). One of the jobs he undertook as an adolescent was to collect signatures for the electoral register and this is how he came to meet a remarkable individual, one of a few who have had a marked influence on the writer's life and work. Having knocked on Dugald Semple's door and requested his signature for the roll, the young White was taken aback when the man refused. Semple invited him in to hear his reasons and there began a long friendship. Dugald Semple was a vegetarian, a naturalist, a transcendentalist and an anarchist, and he had known Gandhi. He possessed a remarkable library, especially for those times, of Eastern literature from which he invited the schoolboy, already a voracious reader and not just from the conventional reading lists, to borrow, particularly the Upanishads, the beginning of 'my awareness of what Pindar calls, "Asia's great space"'. White often speaks of the thrill of confirmation he received upon reading in the Upanishad text the phrase 'You are that' and its implied recognition, which seemed in tune with the experiences and ideas he was living with, that 'personal identity' or the socio-personal context, was inadequate and that a larger identity was knowable through direct relationship with what is out there, 'that'.

Describing this period in his life in an interview[18] White recalls:

> In short, after Christianity, I passed through this hinduising, transcendentalist phase. But pretty soon it also seemed too heavy. My friend was in the habit of launching into great speculations on the after-life, immortality . . . I already felt that all this was not for me. That's when Dugald would say, in a friendly but slightly bemused way, 'you don't believe in anything, do you, Kenneth?'

3. The Glasgow Student

White's evolving experience, embracing the socio-personal context more and more as it had to as he grew older, was pulling him in an opposite direction from the world of the Fairlie moors and shore, back towards the city – Glasgow. Schooled at Largs Higher Grade and Ardrossan Academy, at both of which he was dux, White went on to the University of Glasgow in 1954 to study French and German with subsidiary studies in Latin and Philosophy. This might be an appropriate point at which to examine the sort of country he was stepping into as an adult.

Modern (post-eighteenth century) Scotland had been,

typically, a place to leave. There was more than mere arrogant English ignorance in Dr. Johnson's infamous comment: 'the noblest prospect a Scotsman ever sees is the high road that leads to England'. America was populated by Scots burnt out of their homes in the north by landlords supported by the British State, Australia by political prisoners 'transported' for daring to react against the social and economic oppression of the industrial revolution. Others were forced out of their homes and the independent self-sufficient economy of their cultural history into areas where they would have to turn to waged labour. The agents of the Clearances were quite explicit about this – here in the words of the most notorious of them, Patrick Sellar, in 1815[19]:

> Lord and Lady Stafford were pleased humanely to order a new arrangement of this County. That the interior should be possessed by Cheviot Shepherds and the people brought down to the coast and placed there in lots under the size of three arable acres, sufficient for the maintenance of an industrious family, but pinched enough to cause them to turn their attention to the fishing. I presume to say that the proprietors humanely ordered this, because it was surely a most benevolent action, to put these barbarous hordes into a position where they could better associate together, apply to industry, educate their children, and advance in civilisation.

On the other hand, Scots were not just victims of the economic revolution, many were at the forefront of its advance as leading functionaries of the Empire – soldiers, businessmen, officials, missionaries – people often seen as representing, with dour efficiency, the calvinist tradition of the 'protestant work ethic'.

There had been internal migration also and White's family, as detailed above, had been part of it. The industrial revolution was fuelled by a labour force driven out of the crofting townships of the north into the burgeoning cities, particularly Glasgow, the 'dear green place' which was to become the most potent image of the modern inferno – 'no mean city'. They were joined by Irish immigrants forced out of Ireland by famines induced by British colonial methods. The image of Glasgow became the image of Scotland – industry, invention and enterprise underpinned by a puritan calvinism, sitting alongside the extremes of poverty, squalor, sectarianism and violence. Down the Clyde, on which the great ships of Empire were built, sailed the rich produce of industrial Britain to its export markets, under the eyes of its poverty-ridden workers.

Perhaps a certain kind of self-contradicting culture was bound to develop – the psychology of the victim, the eternal loser, accompanied by a sentimental attachment to dreams and heroes as a refuge from reality. A sense of loss, a terrible yearning, an anger that sometimes boils up to the surface is apparent in so much of the culture which was, and still is to some extent, transmitted to Scots. 'Lament' is a Scots term, and it has been the strain of Scottish upbringing for nearly three hundred years as in the song for the dead at the Battle of Flodden, which took place in 1415 but whose lament was written in the eighteenth century: 'the flooers o the forest are a wede awa'. Then there is the great pipe tune in memory of the family of pipers whose significance was reduced to nothing in the cultural annihilation in the aftermath of Culloden, MacCrimmon's Lament (one of Jock White's favourite pieces):

No more, no more, no more, MacCrimmon
till dawns the sad day of doom and burning
MacCrimmon is here no more returning

More positive expression has taken the form of political idealism (very much the case with White's father) which informed the Scottish contribution to the British radical movements, a contribution which has been, and remains, in theory and practice, of the first significance. Among writers, however, this has often led to a social realism which has, ultimately, had a self-propagating effect on the negative images just described.

The result has been that accumulation of untenable contradictions which is felt to be so acute that it has led to the creation of its very own sobriquet: 'the caledonian antisyzygy'. Briefly, one need only think of the co-existence of remarkable physical beauty, which appears in places to be geologically virgin, Rannoch Moor, say, or the Lewisian gneiss which is three billion years old, coexisting in the mental map of our country with the ultimate industrial squalor of the young White's Glasgow, or of the archetypally Scottish psychological contradiction of the cohabitation of the rational and the fantastic which is presented in James Hogg's *Confessions of a Justified Sinner*, and R. L. Stevenson's *Dr. Jekyll and Mr. Hyde*.

In this Glasgow, with its merchant wealth evident in the magnificent architecture of the centre, especially the buildings of Archibald 'Greek' Thomson and Charles Rennie Mackintosh, its industrial wealth in the cranes and gantries which peopled the skyline above the Clyde shipyards, its cultural wealth in its art galleries and libraries, its rich popular culture focussed on

Glasgow Green, and with its poverty, squalor and violence in the slum areas of the working class upon which all that wealth depended, Kenneth White was to feel as acutely as anyone the tensions of his country's contradictions, but he was to fashion his own solutions to these problems.

He approached his studies with that idiosyncratic individualism which had already established itself in his character as a child, seeing the university not only as a place to work towards a degree but, more importantly, in its libraries, a remarkable resource for his own, self-guided intellectual development. 'I devoured the bookshelves, from theology to mineralogy', he says, and already we see the voracious, encyclopaedic capacity for books which MacDiarmid also possessed. White points to particularly influential authors at this time: Ovid, Rimbaud, Hölderlin, Nietzsche and Heidegger, a mix of poetry and philosophy. Of Scottish writers at this period he speaks of Carlyle, especially his *Sartor Resartus*:

> *In a sinister room in Glasgow*
> *(foghorns sounding along the river)*
> *I'm reading* Sartor Resartus
> *attracted by the figure*
> *of Professor Teufelsdröckh*
> *'diabolical dragon'*
> *Professor of* Allerley-Wissenschaft
> *'all kinds of science'*
> *in the University of* Weissnichtwo
> *'God knows where'*[20]

He talks also of the unique collection of art works, now exhibited as The Burrell Collection, in the Glasgow Art Gallery where, in particular he made acquaintance with Van Gogh whose paintings he did not see as 'part of "art" or "culture"' but as having 'life-value' emanating from their 'aura of energy, a life-force, a kind of luminous ferocity'[21]. He links his introduction to, and contemplation of, Van Gogh's paintings to his own developing sense of himself as artist:

> I had the sensation of transcending national boundaries. I felt I was outside everything, and yet at the heart of reality.

He had a student-writer's room – 'a table strewn with books and papers, bundles of notes pinned to the wall'[22] – in which the exploration of the world's intellectual landscape was underway. From that room he also penetrated the social-historical context in which he was now living – the twentieth century city:

> From that window, in the green dawns and the crimson sunsets, I had it all before my eyes, and in my mind as I trailed the grey streets. Often a creeping yellow fog was part of the scene. You could hear the screech of trams and, in the distance, the horns of ships coming up the sluggish river.[23]

White reveals intense attraction and repulsion in regard to the city he explored obsessively, by day and by night, in much the same way as he did the city's libraries. Glasgow, 'the *id* of Western civilisation'[24] was 'a cancerous spread'[25] but it was full of signs:

> On the south side of the river, in the Gorbals, that had

been Jewish before it became Pakistani, there was a whole Orient: women in multi-coloured saris trailing about the wet mucky streets; and in the local library there were books in Hebrew that made me think of the centres of Hassidism. At the corner of any street, I might have met, in the guise of some old Glaswegian in a murky gaberdine, the Rabbi Elimelekh or the Baal-Shem himself![26]

He sees Glasgow as 'Hell', but, recalling Dostoievski's remark that 'my friend is the whole of St. Petersburg', accepts that Glasgow is such a 'friend' too: 'I am a part of this Hell, I accept its necessity':

> For it *is* hell, there is no doubt about that. The wide streets of this city when the sky is all pinched with cold, or when the drizzle exhales a mist, or when that round red object in the heavens reminds you vaguely of the sun, are hell pure and simple.[27]

But if there is this infernal perspective, explored also in early city poems written by White in the parlance of the streets if not in respectable Lallans, 'The Song of the Coffin Close' or 'The Ballad of the C&W Man'[28]:

> *At last tae get oot frae the stoor 'n stink*
> *ah went aa tae hell an took tae drink*
> *chasin eftir Nothin frae bar tae bar*
> *followin Oblivion's bleary star*

there is also a delight in the sheer energy of the place and the characters of its citizens:

> Glasgow's grotesques. I know hundreds of them. I've
> lived with them. Good God, I'm one of them. Buskers,
> gravediggers, lamplighters, nightwatchmen, railwaymen,
> rag and bone men, coalmen, fly men . . .[29]

Certain signs imprint themselves in his mind and resurface in his writing like the 'noisy bevy of drunken gulls' wheeling round the docks on the Clyde amid the vapours of whisky barrels, the blue sari'd woman on the bridge and the blue Tibetan poppy seen in the Botanic Gardens, the ships 'lit by green light', the 'soft and multiple skies'[30]. If Edinburgh is a classical place, his native city is more oriental: 'If Edinburgh is Athens, Glasgow is China'[31]. Glasgow was 'the old stinking bog out of which, potentially, the lotus could grow'[32].

Again, much of White's writing about this whole period is, of course, retrospective, but one can discern a young man becoming increasingly angry at the sort of world he was living in and the dichotomy which he felt keenly between the 'civilisation' of the city and the reality of the earth awoken in him on the Fairlie moors, while at the same time more and more excited at the intellectual cultural world which his studies were opening up for him.

4. Munich: Isolation and Meditation

In 1956 White was awarded a scholarship at the University of

Munich for a year. One of his professors recommended a break as he was 'showing alarming signs of intellectual unrest'[33]. White himself felt 'a need to distance myself both from my early context and surrounding society'[34].

Munich was another city, less of a 'hell' than Glasgow, but for all its cultural beauty, it represented no answer to the problem of civilisation shaping in his mind and to which he was increasingly formulating a 'barbarian's' answer:

> listening at night
>   to the blind man's radio
>
>   howling
>   knowing every painting in the Haus der Kunst
>   having climbed
>   with my cold barbarian eyes
>   every baroque pillar in the city
>   finding no paradise.[35]

This was White's 'first real experience of life out on my own, with neither stilts nor quilt'[36] and his image of that period reflects this idea of the 'barbarian' outsider ranging the fringes of the city:

> My stay in Munich. Transcendental winter. The wooden shack at the far end of the Englischer Garten, on the edge of town, the green and icy flow of the Isar behind the garden. Grass and bushes gripped by frost. Frozen solitude, then a fragile flowering branch on the plum tree: spring.[37]

Here, during a long icy winter, he was reading German philosophy, especially Nietzsche and Heidegger, but he also renewed his acquaintance with Eastern thought and expression through 'certain Japanese texts (those of Dôgen, Bankei, Hakuin) that hit my brain like lightning'.

One book had a particular effect – *Zen and Japanese Culture* by D. T. Suzuki. White refers to his reading of this book as 'a decisive stage' in his life because, offering a means to release the tension he felt between modern civilisation and the intensity of his experience of land and seascape, a tension which seemed to be resolved for others by religious methods, Suzuki's book indicated the possibility of 'a non-transcendental transcendence', a penetrating awareness of reality but which keeps everything 'at the level of rice and tea, that is, the ordinary'. It is the beginning, perhaps, of the coherence which his 'intellectual unrest' was seeking. Might there be the possibility of maintaining that extreme intensity of feeling and clarification in body and mind that he had experienced in his childhood 'territory', without recourse to the heavy vocabulary of 'religion' and 'the sacred', or the other-worldliness of the 'transcendental'? Might there be an identity which is both 'nirvana and samsara, absolute and existential'? Might we enjoy both *eros* and *logos* at the same time? The sense that this is not only possible but fundamentally necessary in order to achieve the sort of penetration towards reality which he seeks, makes of these questions the beginning of White's habit of creating his own vocabulary:

> Those little words like 'God', 'soul' and 'nation' have done a great deal of harm. That's why I use grotesque words which cannot do any harm to anyone: 'erotocosmology', for example![38]

5. Paris: The Incandescent Zone

Having returned to Glasgow in 1957 to continue his studies, White obtained in 1959 a double first in French and German and was nominated best student in the Faculty of Arts. He was also awarded a postgraduate scholarship. The choice of Paris was immediate.

In Paris he married Marie-Claude Charlut whom he had met in Glasgow where she was working as an assistant and researching into Scottish Literature. Of that small number of people mentioned above who have been of great significance in White's life and work, Marie-Claude must be the most significant of all. Her's is a felt presence, both emotional and intellectual (White has said she is his most demanding critic). Eventually, too, Marie-Claude proved to be a first class translator, becoming in time the sole translator of White's poetry and prose narrative work (he was to write most of his essays directly in French), which gave her a pivotal role in White's itinerary, since it was from the French (sometimes with the adjunct of the original English manuscripts) that his work was translated into other languages.

White's chosen area of research was 'Poetry and Politics' in the context of Surrealism and most of the authors upon whom he concentrated included Surrealists and others working in related areas: André Breton, Antonin Artaud, René Daumal and Henri Michaux. These are writers for whom there is no equivalent, in number and artistic stature, in the English Literature context.

White was, as he says, 'living quite spartanly'[39], earning some extra money by giving private lessons in English. His thesis was fairly quickly abandoned (though not the study of the authors concerned) as the intellectual nomad in him took over as it had done in Glasgow and he began 'wandering round the streets and backstreets of Paris'. However, his Parisian nomadism, although experiencing similar nightmare visions of the endgame of civilisation, feels more confident, seems on surer ground, has more sense of an aim materialising if not yet clearly in view. It is more 'limbo' than 'hell'. As he puts it himself:

> In Glasgow, I was slowly going mad. And now, what am I? An open field.[40]

His experiences in Paris (those first four years and another period later), furnished the material of the manuscript that was to become *Incandescent Limbo*. The Paris he evokes in *Incandescent Limbo* is, like Glasgow, full of 'bizarre, sometimes beautiful encounters, absolute solitudes, dances of the mind'[41], moments of limbo and moments of transcendence:

> For two days I had been in limbo, and there, suddenly, for no apparent reason, I was full of joy [. . .] transported by the feeling of blueness (the sky) and the fresh smell of running water (in the gutter).[42]

It has that combination of humour and penetrating perception which characterises White's prose narrative books as here when, in a freezing, dark room, he cannot get to sleep:

> I have the impression of being a negative in a tank of cold liquid inside a darkroom. Pardon me, Monsieur, is that a metaphor? No, it's a photograph.[43]

But it also contains the nightmare visions of an alienating civilisation and the sense of an individual striving to retain particular significance in the mess of mass urban living. Looking at a sick cat hanging around the street on the lookout for edible rubbish, he recognises, in the 'feverish torpor' of its sick eyes, human beings he has encountered:

> . . . the old woman in the church, the 'poet' who wanted to 'live intensely', the young girl with the long blond hair I met in the underground. All those depressed characters, they spread their vomit over the world – in the name of Religion, Genius, Love, God knows what. It's a mortal sickness. I smell its stench everywhere. For me, nothing but the white world, the world I bring to life by living. And before this world, if necessary, to cure my own sickness, like some other cats I know, a little solitary hole somewhere.[44]

The 'white world' of the Fairlie moors and the Scottish west coast and its islands has become an internalised life force. More than a sense of world beyond the confines of the city, it has become a sense of being which exists beyond the confines of humanism and rationalism, a sense of being which, however, must be defended, and with difficulty:

> Sometimes, seized with panic, I envy those with a niche in the world and in time (profession, family, house), and an idea of the future (even if that just means more of the same thing). Sometimes it happens that I take fright at this peculiar activity of mine, and ask myself if I have not taken a wrong turning.[45]

He remarks on the 'high dose' of self-confidence required,

akin to the Greek 'hybris' or the 'demoniac possession' of Christianity, in a society which cannot support such activity as he is engaged in which has no obvious social purpose. He notes that most 'artists' look to society for approbation, justification, identity, but dismisses such an attitude as 'infantile' and its motivation as 'sucking at success':

> I have never considered myself as 'an artist', defined either as a producer of pabulum for immediate social consumption, or as a public personage in the cultural limelight. In both cases, the artist is caught up in a complex of individual/public relationships, exactly that outside of which I keep myself. In movement, via a process of deconditioning, towards a transpersonal reality.[46]

If White's attempts at deconditioning himself are extreme, his ultimate aims are equally large:

> It is not a reality, the state of things which is ours today. It hasn't the body of a reality, it has neither the fibre nor the tatchiness of a reality. It is a universe of distance and separation, a world where boredom and catastrophe follow each other, deprived of depth and essential continuity. I want real reality. Everything I write is a move towards a little real reality.[47]

The combination of movement and writing which *Incandescent Limbo* presents as the main features of White's experience in Paris is common practice in his life and he emphasises the connection between the two almost to the point of identifying them at a deeper level:

> I am the survivor of a great catastrophe and I am trying
> to re-establish contact. I walk and I write for the same
> reasons. To make the right movements and to renew lost
> relationships.[48]

Reading is another essential element in this process and in Paris White met another influential individual with some similarities to Dugald Semple in Fairlie. Lucien Biton, who features in *Incandescent Limbo* as Maître Léon, was, like Semple, possessed of a remarkable private library which he invited the young Scottish writer to borrow from and discuss on a weekly basis. In a lecture given in Glasgow in 1991, 'Adventures of a Bibliomaniac', White recalls this man and his experiences with him with great affection and humour. They would spend a whole day discussing books and ideas, fuelled initially by coffee and then by white wine, and at the end of it White pictures himself going off into the streets with a dozen books under his arm – 'the week's reading' – which would become the subject of their conversation the following week:

> . . . drinking black coffee and white wine, handling this
> or that book from the ten thousand volumes gathered
> together in his rooms. [. . .] The range of concepts goes
> from the quality of garden peas and passes through all the
> images of 'human imbecility' to arrive at the particular
> dialectic practised at Nalanda.[49]

White's immersion into Eastern philosophy and poetry continued, and the simple sight of the name Shiva in a book was, he says, enough to take him off 'among the giant rhododendrons of the Himalayas', but there was also a sense of 'north' beginning to appear not just in terms of the images and experiences one would expect in a northern writer, but in terms of an intellectual concept as well, borrowed from Nietzsche, but beginning to be developed in his own way:

> I'm always thought of as a Scotsman. But I'm an Eskimo by naturalisation. And this nationality itself is only passport protocol. In fact, I'm a Hyperborean. Nobody knows anything about the Hyperboreans. The Hyperborean is a man out on an erratic path towards a region situated somewhere off the map. People only see the erratics (the stones he leaves in his tracks), but what he sees, in lightning flashes, is the region beyond. No definition is possible of what he sees over there. We're twenty thousand miles from civilisation.[50]

White did not start writing *Incandescent Limbo* from the notes he had kept in Paris until he went to live in Meudon on the outskirts of Paris in 1961. It was not ready for publication for another twelve years after that, and finally saw the light of day as a book, in Paris, in 1976. However, extracts and drafts were published in various French reviews between 1965 and 1975. The first of these publications was in 1965, when White was back in Glasgow, in *Les Lettres Nouvelles* edited by Maurice Nadeau, under the title 'A la lisière du monde' ('On the edge of the world'). White's text was the lead piece in this distinguished French review and, although this was not his first publication, that fact alone was an affirmation of the status already given him. But it was even more important than that, because the text attracted the admiring attention of André Breton, who wrote to White[51] that he had been 'struck by its high accent of originality', and congratulated the magazine's editor for showing 'great discernment, indeed foresight, in placing this text at the head of the issue'. Breton had also received a copy of *En toute candeur*, the book of autobiographical sketches and poems published by Pierre Leyris at the famous house of the Mercure de France in 1964, and he has this to say of it:

> I am far from exhausting its powers. It requires to be tasted very patiently – as I found was the case with the poetry of Trakl.

This reception from leading French and European literary figures – to Breton we can add the poet René Char and the philosopher E. M. Cioran – was not to find its equivalent, except for some far-sighted individuals, in Britain where White's work puzzled rather than enthused. It is important to bear in mind, when looking at the British literary and cultural context and White's response to it, that he had with him, from an early point in his writing career, the confirmation of some of the best literary minds in Europe.

6. Gourgounel: Resourcing

In 1961, White bought, for next to nothing, an old abandoned farmhouse, Gourgounel – in a region of south-east France, the Ardèche. He explains in the preface to the first French edition of

Lettres de Gourgounel that after two years in the city of Paris he felt 'like an exile' and had looked for

> a place of emptiness [. . .] to concentrate my life and thought. I found it in the Ardèche, more precisely, in the valley of the Beaume, in the hamlet of Praduches, at a place called Gourgounel (that name gurgled, it spoke the language of sources).[52]

In this 'hermit's kingdom' which spoke 'only of the essential – solitude, silence, wind, sun and storm'[53] – White combined the physical work of turning the abandoned farm into a liveable space, with mental work of study and writing, especially about his experiences in the Ardèche. After the teeming life of the city Gourgounel's emptiness wasn't only a delight but a space to explore:

> In Paris everything had been going round in circles, amidst a confusion which was nauseating. In that context, I began to feel more and more separated from myself as well as others and the only place where I am not at all alone is precisely in this solitude.[54]

If *Incandescent Limbo* is a book of ice cold winter with aurora borealis flashes, *Letters from Gourgounel* is a book of burning sun and summer lightning. The thunderstorm at the centre of the book, 'a field of energy' in the world, centred round the presence of the Tanargue, the chain of mountains facing Gourgounel, gathers and breaks in a parallel to the enlightenment which gathers and breaks in White's mind through intellectual penetration and live experience of the environment:

In this region the people say: '*lou troun toumbo oqui vounté sen dévé*' (lightning strikes where it must). That's the place for me to be.[55]

There is much emphasis in the book on the correlation of the physical and the mental. The earth provides food for the grateful body: from the little goat cheeses of the farm to the mushrooms and blueberries of the forest, not forgetting the wines of the little monastery of Our Lady of the Snows, a place which White was to discover had also been a favourite source of 'smoking bottles' for a predecessor in these regions, Robert Louis Stevenson (about whose presence in the Ardèche he was to write a book years later). This is no get-back-to-the-land idea, rather there is a developing sense of the falsity in the dualism which underpins modern culture – the separation of the human from the earth, of the mind from the body, and the aim is something so unconventional, inhabitual and unexpressed as a new grounding of being:

I do not know what the builders of society have in store for us, but I think that, whatever the number of super-motorways, super-markets, super-factories, super-space-rockets etc. with which the future will be laden, there will always be individuals who will want to return from time to time to the back country (let's hope there will still be one) and [. . .] gather blueberries, that is, savour a little of the taste of the earth-ground.[56]

This last sentiment is not a return to nature romanticism, rather it is an indicator of the focus of a new way of thinking, the grounding of a new culture. And White's thoughts also turn to the expression of this new perspective. He works on translating Chinese and Japanese poetry[57], seeking a 'freshness' of language which he finds missing in the 'poetic' style favoured by the translators he is reading. In this translation of a haiku by Buson:

> *Contemplate! the sea undulates in spring*
> *and undulates all day long*

he cuts out a 'grandiloquent' word such as 'contemplate' and replaces it with the simple exclamation, 'Ah!', the 'dead' word 'undulate' is removed, the text being given instead an undulating rhythm partly achieved by repetition but also by the economy and simplicity of expression achieved by the changes:

> *Ah! the waves of the sea in spring*
> *waves of the sea in spring*
> *all day long*

Similarly:

> *The sea is angry! The Milky Way extends*
> *above as far as the Isle of Sado*

becomes, in White's reworking:

> *Angry sea*
> *and beyond as far as Sado*
> *the Milky Way!*

This simplicity and purity of language becomes increasingly

part of White's own writing at this time to join another aspect which, already present, is reinforced by his reading of the great Chinese artist and poet Wang Wei – the presence of 'world' achieved by 'a state of mind liberated from anxiety, [. . .] a mental landscape in harmony with the landscape outside':

> He speaks of 'world' and makes a distinction between a poet who 'creates world' and those who are content to describe the state of things, just as he distinguishes poetry which 'has world' from that which does not.[58]

And on the same subject of Wang Wei:

> This is about neither idealism nor realism. It is perhaps about allowing deep sensations to reach the highest areas of the brain, where they may be deployed in an emptiness which is a plenitude.[59]

This 'sense of world', the constant theme of White's work, was also being felt at the everyday levels of existence. After years of studying French and now living in France he links his growing linguistic world to the expanding world of his experience and his ideas:

> Not only was I navigating more and more easily between two languages but, starting from these two languages, I had the feeling I was approaching a universal language the way the Dordogne and the Garonne meet to form La Gironde and mix their waters with those of the Atlantic Ocean.[60]

7. First Publications

From 1962 to 1963 White taught English literature at the Sorbonne in Paris. During this time he became a published poet, his students in 'Le Club des Étudiants d'Anglais' publishing his first collection *Wild Coal*.

One can see in this first book some formal conventionalism with rhymes and metric regularity and occasional inversion as well as poems in the forms of ballads, sonnets and poems in Scots. The dialectic between city and earth, between the social world and the intensity of personal experience which his childhood had developed, is explored in these pages through the voice of a poet more personally present than in later work, clearly an angry figure but also one seeking a more fulfilling sense of reality. The fundamental images are there such as the gull, the sea, tree, hill and rock, but approached sometimes in a quasi-religious way as in 'Precentor Seagull' with its 'archangel of language'. Nevertheless, there is a formal assuredness and a confidence of expression, which is striking in such a young poet. The desire for an intensity of 'life-force' which combines eros and logos is exuberantly present throughout and breaks out towards the sort of naked clarity evident in White's later work:

> squawking! squawking!
> no voice of dumb eternity yours
> but a barbary tongue firm-cased
> in flesh and bone
> alive and antic
> grotesque and graceful[61]

In some of the poems, such as 'Morning Walk' quoted above, that sense of reality begins to manifest itself in its own right and in its own necessary form of expression.

It was after the publication of *Wild Coal* that the editor of the English language section at the French publishers, Mercure de France, Pierre Leyris, translator of T. S. Eliot and Hopkins, wrote to White saying he was 'greatly moved' by his poems. He invited White to write some biographical material, his 'personal mythology'[62], to accompany Leyris' translations of White's poems for a book, *En toute candeur*, which went into their English literature catalogue. White was the only living writer to appear in that list, yet another indication of the mark his work was making.

In this book, White takes the opportunity to explore his background in three essays. The first, 'The Matricial Hills', deals with the sea and moors of Fairlie. He writes of a poetry which is not 'nature poetry' but 'earth poetry' and is already aware that his sense of an earth culture which he feels in the Scottish landscape is linked to a global space:

> . . . my greatest space of being is perhaps that crown of the world which goes from Scotland to Iceland and Alaska, and comes down again by Siberia into China, Japan and India. I've heard tell of a Eurasian circumpolar civilisation, of a prehistoric arctic and sub-arctic civilisation. We know very little about this yet, and many of its vestiges could be lying deep below the ice, but I feel that that is the culture I ultimately belong to.[63]

The characteristic expressions of his vision of poetry are also already present:

Poetry could be a little white dawn[64]

and

Poetry is existential plenitude[65]

The second essay, 'Hell's Blazes', explores his family background and the city of Glasgow, 'where dragons proliferate – and sing!'[66].

In the third essay, entitled 'The White World', he presents the sort of poetry, 'both abstract and naturalist'[67] he is seeking, a writing which will 'rediscover cosmos – a world of beauty and order (chaotic order)', a poetry which will, as T. S. Eliot had argued earlier in the century, 'return to prose' – a world-bearing prose. For him, poetry is not a matter of versifying, it is 'primordial, existing before literature'. This, again, does not imply any backward step towards some kind of noble savage illusion, rather it implies 'penetrating through to a reality' overlain by layers of secondary discourse, false ideas, confused perception.

Poetry is a matter of reality-content and of rhythm, not the rhythm of metrics, but the rhythm of the earth, the cosmos:

> For a sense of rhythm, it is better to get someone to walk along the shore on a windy day than to teach him versification.[68]

Already White is aware of something which will become more and more profoundly part of his poetics and which, as we shall see, he will find confirmed in his future intellectual nomadising among the literatures of the world, that 'rhythm and language are in fact cosmological long before they are literary'[69].

Here, the 'sense of world' does not only cover the idea, still a radical one in today's more 'ecologically conscious' age, that 'world' means much more than the human context, it brings in the idea that expression also is not simply confined to the human:

> The rhythm of the greatest poetry is not only that of human language (which itself has more resources than simple literary form), but that of the cosmos.[70]

The poet, as understood by our society, is, according to this perspective, for the most part, not a poet at all because the would-be poet has not only 'lost affinity with the cosmos'[71], but has no notion of what this means and implies. The poet evoked by White has more to do with what in previous societies was a religious figure, or a philosopher-figure, or, going further back, a shaman-figure. Similarly, the social preoccupations of modern society and its writers miss the mark:

> It is not communication between man and man that matters, but communication between man and cosmos. Put men in contact with the cosmos, and they will be in contact with one another.[72]

In other words, the apparently egocentric, individualist programme being announced in *En toute candeur*, has an ultimate social objective but is seeking to reach it not by the political or collective way, but through the promulgation of a larger 'sense of world' and a larger sense of 'identity' which do not occasion pascalian panic, but a sense of liberation and independence which will make social relations more natural therefore stronger. Real artists 'enlarge the sense of life' – the word 'author', as White points out, being derived from the Latin *augere*, to 'augment' – but this implies a stage of struggle and suffering which most people prefer to avoid, thus remaining in the apathy engendered by false belief or the miserable indulgence of despair:

> To possess a live sense of life and to attain to deep consciousness of self, is to go from dependence – a state which most never leave – to existence, in a world which becomes a provocation. The world is a provocation to me. Over against it, I evoke my own world, which is a more real world. Poetry is affirmation of reality. No more, no less.[73]

The implications of all this are wide-ranging and I shall return to them, and the way White develops them, later. At the moment it is worth noticing that this young writer (White is twenty-seven when he is writing these words) has turned his back on most of what passes for 'literature' and has worked out for himself the ground of what he considers to be a larger poetics from which he will take off on a journey of experience and expression, which will largely confirm the intuitions being voiced here, and will lead to a type of poetry and prose writing which is quite unique in Scotland and beyond.

8. On the British Literary Scene

White came back to Scotland in 1963, feeling that he had 'unfinished business'. While working in the French department at the University of Glasgow, teaching by choice the pre-revolutionary Encyclopedists (Diderot, Voltaire, Rousseau), and modern French poetry since Rimbaud, he also started up the Jargon Group, devoted to what he called 'cultural revolution'. Exactly what White meant by 'cultural revolution' will be gone into in more detail in the second part of this book.

A book of poems, *The Cold Wind of Dawn*, and the prose book, *Letters from Gourgounel*, were published simultaneously by Jonathan Cape in London in 1966, to be followed soon (in 1968) by another book of poems, *The Most Difficult Area*, and two books of translation: one, a selection of André Breton's poems, the other, Breton's long poem 'Ode to Charles Fourier', accompanied by a substantial essay by White on utopian socialism.

The poems in *The Cold Wind of Dawn* gather together the poems previously published in Paris and new work where the power of the poet's intensifying relationship with landscape is dominating the poems from the social context and the city.

The religious tone and references are still present here and there ('apostles of rain', 'this holy-of-holy rock'). The influence of Gerard Manley Hopkins, important to the poet still in the theoretical terms of 'inscape' and 'instress' and an inspirational model for his attachment to arpeggio-like word-coining and original and surprising uses of syntax, is audible in some of the poetic expression. But what strikes most is a range of poeticality that goes from the sheer sensuous lyricism of the 'Poem of the White Hare', which reads like the leap of imaginative intelligence into live phenomenology:

> *A thought that leaped out like a hare*
> *over the moor, from behind a great rock*
> *oh, it was a white leaping hare, and*
> *the heather was a fine red world*
> *for its joyance, just that day on the moor*
> *a grey day marching on the winds*
> *into winter, a day for a sparkling sea*
> *three miles away in the trough of the islands*
> *a day high up at the end of the year*
> *a silence to break your heart, oh*
> *the white hare leaping, see the white hare.*[74]

through the humorous touches of 'Irish Rain':

> *Mother of mine for five days now*
> *this heart has been smoking thick black melancholy*
>
> *the rain is running down every hump*
> *and there's not a bit of yellow sun in sight*
>
> *I sit scraping away at this deal table*
> *like an old angel trying to learn the fiddle.*[75]

and the jazzy tonality, with its concrete image of dockside cranes, that we find in 'Glasgow Night':

> *In the world there is fog*
> *and rain*

> *and mud*
> *and grease*
> *and stench*
> *that's the cargo that Glasgow*
> *unloads on my mind*
> *and this night it's all there:*
> > *the fog*
> > *the rain*
> > *the mud*
> > *the grease*
> > *the stench*
> *while I improvise a lonely blues*
> *to which the boats contribute*
> *boat that comes up the river*
> *boat that goes down the river*
> *fog-horns in action*
> *the one sounding:* glas
> *the other:* gow
> *as though the city*
> *were blowing trombone*
> *ready to jazz with the sea.*[76]

into the starkness of the series of winter poems such as 'Near Winter', with its sensations of an archaic, primal Scotland, 'Winter World', with its cold, lucid vision, 'The Winter of the World', with its medieval tonality.

The final poem, 'Solstice', with its epigraph from Villon evoking the life of wolves in winter, lays out a programme of living and working:

> Give yourself room for a real beginning
> the man who works in a narrow space

builds no more than prison or grave.[77]

In the course of that wildly extravagant poem 'Solstice', White says: 'I have lived in the Chinese mountains/and planted bamboo in drizzling rain', and at least one poem resonates with Chinese references, like those, as we have seen, to be found explicitly in *Letters from Gourgounel*:

LIVING IN THE HILLS

The road I came by climbs by nine thousand feet
the river I crossed has many waterfalls
the path to the house is steep and narrow
in summer the brambles seal it off
in winter I stare out over the valley
the snow falls thickly through its darkness
I look in the fire and think it a dream
that once I lived in the streets of a city.[78]

Reviewers welcomed these books and they tended to place White as a phenomenon apart, on the margins of the British literary scene.

Writing in *The Sunday Times*[79], Maurice Wiggin saw White as standing outside 'the main stream or rather muddy eddy' of contemporary British literature, heralding something as yet undefined. This was clairvoyant, but didn't go far into definition.

In his book *The Truth of Poetry*[80], Michael Hamburger puts White alongside Saint-John Perse and Paul Celan, calling him a 'post-Nietzschean', which, as critical vocabulary, sounds promising, going far beyond the usual 'I like, I don't like'. But this definition is made in a chapter entitled 'Town and Country', that is, in a context vaguely Georgian and sounding like some weekend magazine, which, to say the least, is inadequate. Hamburger thereafter goes on to criticise White's radical naturalism (it is bare, that is, neither 'mystic' nor 'occult') and reproach him for having no social or religious idealism, no 'ideas of the good city'. If this was all Britain could do by way of philosophical criticism, one could understand White's feeling a certain amount of impatience.

More and more he was going to adopt an inner distance, within which he advanced his work. It's the winter poems that lead him to the book with the significant title *The Most Difficult Area*.

This book begins with a poem 'Prose of the White-Haired Seagulls', which is an invocation to the Rosy Gull: 'In the arctic winter, when all other birds go south, the Rosy Gull heads north and winters probably in the very central parts of the Polar Sea.' The whole book is concerned with the notion of limit, silence, monotony, emptiness, all of those approaching that 'area' which he would be exploring both in depth and in extension over the years to come.

As for *Letters from Gourgounel*, Maurice Wiggin called it 'a curiosity of literature', saying that it should have all the success of a bestseller of the time, *Ring of Bright Water*, while being a much deeper book. The literary director at Jonathan Cape had also thought he had the possible makings of a bestseller, if White would only add a few more anecdotal bits, which White declined to do. When White presented his second prose book to Cape, a book even 'further out than the *Letters*'[81] (it was an earlier version of *Incandescent Limbo*) he was advised to write a novel, maybe a social realist novel about Glasgow, in order to establish his reputation. Again, White said he'd rather not. The situation was clear, both as to the blocked context of Britain and to the fast evolving nature of White's work and thought.

To come back to larger perspectives and finer analyses, in his *Times* article, the critic Maurice Wiggin had made an interesting comparison between Kenneth White and Colin Wilson. Wilson's book, *The Outsider*, had appeared in 1956, to be followed a year later by *Religion and the Rebel*. In comparison with White's, Wilson's thinking is rather woolly, and it was going to lose itself in occult back-alleys. But at least Wilson was addressing issues and following the trajectories of individuals endowed with energy and insight away beyond the normal social and literary scene. Wilson's basic definition of the outsider as the man out to 'extend his range of consciousness' applies perfectly to White. Most of Wilson's modern examples were European: Nietzsche, Van Gogh, Rilke, Camus, the only English language outsiders he could bring in being Joyce and the two Lawrences (D. H. and T. E.). White had read Joyce in Glasgow (*Dubliners, Ulysses, Finnegans Wake*), *The Seven Pillars of Wisdom* was a book whose first paragraph and certain subsequent desert scenes had delighted him, and if he found D. H. Lawrence's theories boring and was often put off by his 'chattering Englishness', he loved books such as *Twilight in Italy* and *Mornings in Mexico*. As to Nietzsche, Rilke and Camus, he knew them thoroughly, and he was later to write a book on Van Gogh. In short, in his work and in his life, White was going to take this whole line with him and attempt to develop a more coherent field.

9. The Departure

In an essay first published in *La Figure du Dehors* ('The Outward Movement') as 'Après Rimbaud'[82], White evokes the crisis point to which his life was heading in these years in Glasgow:

> It was a winter of the mind. A cold wind was blowing from the cosmos. Nietzsche had talked about the death of God . . . Less mythologically, less religiously put, what was going on was the last throes of a metaphysically-based culture.

His intellectual questing had taken him to points which others were not yet ready to follow in Britain, where thought forms he considered totally inadequate were too entrenched:

> The cultural revolution [. . .] must begin [. . .] by sweeping clear the terrain, which implies a radical questioning of two things: humanism (with its by-product, sentimental humanitarianism), and rationalism (with its by-product, blethering ratiocination).[83]

In 1967 White left Scotland again for France. His valedictory note was a long poem entitled 'Walking the Coast' of which he had this to say in Duncan Glen's review *Akros* in which extracts appeared:

> Without a strong prose background, and without a developed philosophical discourse, or at least a constellation of terms within that prose background, poetry

(which is not 'philosophical' but implies a direct encounter
with *sophia*, or 'knowledge') degenerates into a sentimental
bog, or a noisy fairground, or mere intellectualist
conversation, or a linguistic scrambling about in the void
(once the background is gone, pseudo-original growths
proliferate, encumbering and stifling the cultural
landscape) . . . Part of the aim of this poem is to get back
into the background.[84]

Its bold opening, in lines using an open form visually
reminiscent of William Carlos Williams, Ezra Pound and Charles
Olson, and aurally reminiscent of the later MacDiarmid,
declares he has returned to 'the question':

> *for the question is always*
> *how*
> *out of all the chances and changes*
> *to select*
> *the features of real significance*
> *so as to make*
> *of the welter*
> *a world that will last.*[85]

'Exploration, explanation, expression' is a later summation of
what is here, in embryonic form, the geopoetic field. The whole
tone has become more confident, full of verve and free, quick
movement. The poem paints imagistic pictures of the poet's life
so far and refers to some of the main influences: the natural ones
of seascape and moor, with gulls, skuas, herons, trees, flowers
and stones; those coming in from Scottish literature
(MacDiarmid, Urquhart, Duncan Ban, Rob Donn . . .): more
general ones concerning art, science, poetics and philosophy. All

of these have become signs of a world, examples of a method and images of poetic expression. The picture of the lighthouse in section 5 gives a factual account of the edifice in a tone very reminiscent of MacDiarmid but with a sense of formal composition, coherence and completeness which the earlier poet often failed to achieve:

> *and outside in the darkness*
> > *the island lighthouse*
> *a white tower*
> > *36 feet high*
> *with the focal plane 90 feet*
> > > *above high water*
> > *showing a white group-flashing light*
> *with the characteristic*
> > *of 2 flashes in quick succession*
> *every 30 seconds*
> > *its effective intensity*
> *being 200.000 candlepower*
> > *its range in clear weather*
> > > *16 miles.*[86]

This is a poet who has developed a much more complex intuition of poetry than the one current. It is clear in the role being given to rhythm as opposed to metrics and formal convention, and evidenced in the verse's success in uniting content and expression in original ways. The rhythm of the last two lines, bringing the section to a close by opening out the lighthouse's illumination onto the surrounding world, resolves the apparent randomness and formlessness of the previous lines into an overall coherence – the various facts about the lighthouse cohere into its function but that function, while closing the section, opens out in a quiet but clearly affirmative way: 'its range in clear weather / 16 miles'. The lighthouse is the corollary of the poet 'making of the welter a world that will last', its light the corollary of the '200.000 candlepower' poem. Michèle Duclos' description of the poem and the itinerary of the poet which it presents is most apt:

> . . . a dynamic which comes and goes from the centre to the circumference of phenomenal life, the thought of the poet goes from the surface of these very phenomena, ('welter', 'random'), to an organisation or at least a distribution ('pattern') which is more ordered ('world', 'cosmos'), through the use of language ('word'). This is the major problematic of *Walking the Coast*, echoed in a recurrent dynamic from obscurity to light, from complex to simple, from walking movement to contemplation.[87]

The poet talks of 'the biological aim of art', an understanding that poetics imply more than artifice, a principle which is crucial to White's conception and practice – there is affirmation that 'within life there is life'. Also the figures of intellectual nomadism which will occupy White for years begin to appear:

> *living in obscurity*
> > *like Hakuyu*
> *his name meant*
> > *White Obscurity*
> > *his name meant*
> > > *he who lived in the hills*
> *back of Northern White Water –*
> *or secretly though not unconsciously*

> *in the cities of Europe*
> *living my life*
> > *founding and grounding*
> *a world.*[88]

Geological processes become images of the intellect, rocks the image of the poetic expression of that intellect in its highest order, like rosy quartz or 'the blaze of white granite' running through the 'outcrop of dark grey sandstone'.

So, 'Walking the Coast' sums up White's *itinerarium mentis* and expresses his impression of having gone beyond his historical conditioning, as well as the contemporary sociological context, and to have found the main lines of his own geography:

> *and now the struggle at the centre is over*
> > *the circumference*
> > > *beckons from everywhere.*[89]

NOTES

For the convenience of the reader, references for poems in earlier volumes will be made also to the collected *Open World*, which was not available to Tony McManus during the composition of this book. A similar updating will be done for the essays in *The Wanderer and his Charts*. (Editor's note.)

1. In the book *En toute candeur*. The original English version of these essays, translated into French by Pierre Leyris, have not been published as yet.

2. *À ma mère – 60 écrivains parlent de leur mère*, Paris, Éditions Pierre Horay, 1988, p. 369–374. Translation by Tony McManus.

3. *Pilgrim of the Void*, p. 29.

4. *Handbook for the Diamond Country*, p. 118. Taken up again, in a longer sequence entitled 'Haiku of the Sud-Express', in *Open World, Collected Poems* 1960–2000, p. 211–212.

5. This is in a long poem, 'Le testament du littoral', which constitutes the third part of the bilingual *Les Rives du silence*. Not taken up in *Open World*.

6. Translated, in a slightly abridged form, by Kenneth White for Tony McManus from *L'Esprit nomade*, p. 79. An English version of the same essay will be found in *The Wanderer and his Charts*, p. 169–181.

7. 'Scotland, History and the Writer', in *On Scottish Ground*, p. 152.

8. *Handbook for the Diamond Country*, p. 48. *Open World*, p. 3.

9. In *The Bird Path*, p. 41–74. *Open World*, p. 127–179.

10. In various autobiographical pieces published in magazines, and in books of interviews such as *Coast to Coast*, *Le*

Poète cosmographe, *Le Lieu et la Parole*.

11. 7 July 1997.

12. In *The Bird Path*, p. 123–127. *Open World*, p. 598–602.

13. In a special number of the review *Incisions, Incisions III*, entitled 'Le Nouveau Paysage' ('The New Landscape'), Écassines, December 1981, in which texts by White juxtapose others by the painter Michel Moy. The dialogue is taken up again in *Le Poète cosmographe*. The passage quoted here is translated from the French by Tony McManus. White's essay has not yet been published as a whole in English.

14. *Les Rives du silence*, p. 262.

15. 'A Shaman Dancing on the Glacier', in *On Scottish Ground*, p. 36.

16. This and the following two quotations are from the third autobiographical essay in *En toute candeur*, p. 60 and 63. Quoted from the original English manuscripts.

17. 'Morning Walk', in *Handbook for the Diamond Country*, p. 17. *Open World*, p. 58.

18. See 'La dimension cachée', in *Le Lieu et la Parole*.

19. See Eric Richards, *Patrick Sellar and the Highland Clearances*, Edinburgh U. P., 2000.

20. Section 6 of the long poem 'Le Testament du littoral', in Les *Rives du silence*.

21. *Van Gogh and Kenneth White*, p. 61, as for the following quotation.

22. *Les Limbes incandescents*, p. 123. The page numbers for this book refer to the new Denoël edition of 1990. Quoted from White's original English manuscript.

23. *Van Gogh and Kenneth White*, p. 2.

24. See 'Time on a Dark River', in *Travels in the Drifting Dawn*.

25. *Van Gogh and Kenneth White*, p. 2.

26. See 'Rimbaud, Glasgow and Ways West', in the special number of *Chapman* (n° 59, 1990) devoted to the work of Kenneth White. Essay later taken up in *The Wanderer and his Charts*, p. 17–22.

27. Autobiographical essay, 'Les fournaises de la ville', in *En toute candeur*. English text from original manuscript.

28. The early Glasgow poems of *The Cold Wind of Dawn* were taken up, at least some of them, in the 'sociocultural extravaganza for several voices, a tin whistle, a Jew's harp and a sense of supernihilism' entitled 'The Ballad of Kali Road', in *Open World*, p. 24–33.

29. 'Les fournaises de la ville', in *En toute candeur*, p. 49.

30. Quotations from various poems and texts throughout White's writings.

31. 'The Inhabitant of Edinburgh', *Travels in the Drifting Dawn*, p. 63.

32. 'The Big Rain at Tigh Geal', *Travels in the Drifting Dawn*, p. 135.

33. From the notice in the compendium, *World Authors*.

34. Interview 'La dimension cachée', in *Le Lieu et la parole*, p. 88.

35. Section 23 of the long poem 'Walking the Coast', in *The Bird Path*, p. 42–74. *Open World*, p. 125–179.

36. 'La dimension cachée', *Le Lieu et la parole*, p. 88.

37. *Les Limbes incandescents*, p. 87. Quoted from White's original English manuscript.

38. 'La dimension cachée', *Le Lieu et la parole*, p. 91.

39. *On Scottish Ground*, p. 35. As for the quotations following.

40. *Les Limbes incandescents*, p. 145. Quoted from White's original English manuscript, as for the following quotations.

41. *Ibid.*, p. 13.

42. *Ibid.*, p. 104.

43. *Ibid.*, p. 34.

44. *Ibid.*, p. 36.

45. *Ibid.*, p. 110.

46. *Idem.*

47. *Ibid.*, p. 22.

48. *Ibid.*, p. 76.

49. *Ibid.*, p. 134.

50. *Ibid.*, p. 50–51.

51. A letter from André Breton to Kenneth White dated '*Paris, le 10 janvier 1965*', in Kenneth White's personal archives. Translated by Kenneth White for Tony McManus.

52. In *Lettres de Gourgounel* as published by Les Presses d'aujourd'hui in Paris, 1979. This French version was considerably different from the original English edition published by Jonathan Cape, London, in 1966, with some chapters dropped and others added. The current French edition, published by Éditions Grasset in Paris (coll. 'Les Cahiers rouges'), dates from 1986. The revised version of the book has not yet appeared in English. All quotations from *Lettres de Gourgounel* are from the French edition of 1986. This quotation is from p. 16.

53. *Ibid.*, p. 38.

54. *Ibid.*, p. 81.

55. *Ibid.*, p. 39.

56. *Ibid.*, p. 20.

57. *Ibid.*, p. 173–175.

58. *Ibid.*, p. 102–103.

59. *Ibid.*, p. 103.

60. This is from the preface to a translation into English by Kenneth White of Tristan Corbière's text, *Le Casino des trépassés*, published by La TILV (Tribune internationale des langues vivantes), Paris and Perros-Guirec, 1994.

61. The poem from which this extract is taken, 'Precentor Seagull', stands at the head of this first book of White's, *Wild Coal*, published in Paris in 1963. It was taken over as head-poem in *En toute candeur*, and in *The Cold Wind of Dawn*. Thereafter, White dropped it, leaving it out from *The Bird Path*. Not in *Open World* either.

62. Letter from Pierre Leyris in Kenneth White's personal archives.

63. *En toute candeur*, 'Les collines matricielles', p. 36.

64. *Ibid.*, p. 21.

65. *Ibid.*, p. 31.

66. *En toute candeur*, 'Les fournaises de la ville', p. 41.

67. *En toute candeur*, 'Le monde blanc'. All the quotations in this paragraph are from pages 63 and 64.

68. *Ibid.*, p. 66.

69. *Ibid.*, p. 65

70. *Ibid.*, p. 67.

71. *Ibid.*, p. 68.

72. *Idem.*

73. *Ibid.*, p. 69.

74. *The Cold Wind of Dawn*, p. 18.

75. *Ibid.*, p. 16.

76. *Ibid.*, p. 31.

77. *Ibid.*, p. 60.

78. *Ibid.*, p. 40.

79. 20 February 1966.

80. Michael Hamburger, 'Tensions in Modern Poetry from Baudelaire to the 1960s', *The Truth of Poetry*, Harmondsworth, Penguin Books, 1970.

81. White, in conversation.

82. Reprinted in *Chapman* n°59, 1990, as "Rimbaud, Glasgow and Ways West", and, thereafter, in *The Wanderer and his Charts*, 2004.

83. Kenneth White, *Le Monde d'Antonin Artaud*, p. 166.

84. *Akros*, vol. 8, n° 23, December 1973, p. 11. Taken up, in French, in *Une stratégie paradoxale*, as 'Le long du grand rivage'.

85. 'Walking the Coast', in *The Bird Path*, p. 42. *Open World*, p. 127.

86. *Ibid.*, p. 44. *Open World*, p. 131.

87. From a thesis defended by Michèle Duclos at the University of Grenoble in 1993. Published in book form as *Kenneth White, nomade intellectuel, poète du monde*, Grenoble, Ellug, 2006. English translation of excerpts by Tony McManus.

88. 'Walking the Coast', in *The Bird Path*, p. 53. *Open World*, p. 146.

89. *Ibid.*, p. 58. *Open World*, p. 154.

PART TWO:
THE EMERGENT FIELD

So much literature just describes the prison, or comments on it, or has somebody gripping at the bars and howling – or maybe painting the bars in pretty or lurid colours. What I wanted to do was break the cage.

KENNETH WHITE,
On Scottish Ground

1. A Scottish Constellation

The evidence of White's Scottish affinities is both linguistic and philosophical.

If he rarely uses Lallans in a systematic way, he will insert bits of Lallans and Gaelic words and phrases on occasion into his English. As to the nature of that English, it is unmistakably Scottish, both phonetically and rhythmically, and White will indulge himself from time to time in such hyper-Scottish linguistic practices, in the English, as the Ecclefechan style of Carlyle or the Scoto-Babylonian dialect of Urquhart of Cromarty. He illustrates in his own way a kind of Scoto-Celtic linguistic exuberance, grammatical and lexical, that crops up throughout Scottish literature.

As to content and perspective, if the two terms that come first to mind to define White's trajectory and field are 'intellectual nomadism' and 'geopoetics', and if it is certain that he has developed them to an unprecedented extent, it is possible to say that the 'intellectual nomad' is a Scottish type, and that in certain figures White recognises as brothers-in-spirit, road-companions, from Duns Scot to D'Arcy Thompson, via Buchanan and Robert Louis Stevenson, there are elements of at least proto-geopoetics.

One of the figures who offer the most obvious parallel with White's itinerary is George Buchanan (1506–1582). Born 'in the county of Lennox', evidence suggests that Buchanan's native languages were Gaelic and Scots. In 1326, Bishop Murray had established a Collège des Ecossais in Paris with a distinctive 'Scottish Nation', and such was the political and cultural intimacy of the early sixteenth century that France and Scotland were almost one. A formidable number of Scots studied, and, indeed, taught at the Scots college, among them Boyce and Mair, and, eventually, Buchanan. Like his predecessors, he was renowned as a teacher, both in Paris and in Bordeaux, where the significance of his role as tutor to the great French essayist, Montaigne, is emphasised by Kenneth White in his study of the Scottish Latinist.[1] White also points out Buchanan's poetic aim, which chimes with his own, 'to get literature out of the "bog" (Buchanan's expression) of Miracles and Moralities'. As a poet in Latin he is constantly judged as without his equal by his European contemporaries. Indeed, even Pope Urban VIII, though judging him a heretic, was compelled to compliment the Scottish master's Latin version of the Psalms, and felt, as Irving tells it, "'Twas pity it was written by so great a heretic, for otherwise it should have been sung in all churches under his authority.'[2]

On the social plane, Buchanan had no time for authority *per se*. An anecdote tells of how the Countess of Mar remonstrated with him after he had 'chastised' his pupil, the future King James VI, whereupon Buchanan replied, 'Madam, I have whipt his arse, you may kiss it if you please.' On the political plane, for Buchanan, 'all power derives from the people' and, in pursuing that argument, he puts limits on the monarchy and promotes the rights of the people to resist poor kings in such a way as to diminish the concept of primogeniture, a concept alien to the

Celts for whom, in theory at least, the King was the elect of the people, not just the son of the last one. Buchanan's political writings, especially the *De Juri Regni apud Scotos*, in Irving's words, 'established political science on its genuine basis', the basis of freedom, and he states, 'it has taught modern philosophers to discuss the principles of political science with new freedom and energy'.

Buchanan's most ambitious work, however, comes in the line of Erigena's *Periphyseon* and is of clear interest to White in the largeness of its scope – the cosmological poem *De Sphera*, written in five (uncompleted) books, in which Buchanan sought to describe the workings of the universe. That the Ptolemaic system he expounds in his poem was wrong is of less interest here than the great expansive ambition the poem embodies, accompanied by close attention to descriptive detail of the natural world.

Another Scottish intellectual nomad and 'precursor' of White's geopoetics, was Patrick Geddes, to whom White devoted an essay in *On Scottish Ground*.[3]

Botanist and biologist by formal and informal education, Geddes was uncomfortable with the established interpretation of Darwin's theory of evolution as promulgated by Huxley with whom he worked in London, the interpretation summed up in the phrase 'survival of the fittest', which appears to give priority to competition and aggression in the evolution of forms. In his reading of Herbert Spencer's *Principles of Biology*, Geddes found confirmation of his own intuition that co-operation was at least as important a part of the evolutionary process as competition. Geddes went to work in Brittany and from there made for Paris, in the passing making an important discovery which confirmed his intuition regarding Darwinism and is not without relevance to our context here, that the basic substance of plant life – chlorophyll – exists in some forms of animal life.

In France, Geddes found his intellectual home and the two major influences on his thinking: Frédéric Le Play (whose sociological formula 'Place-Family-Work' was taken over by Geddes' 'Place-Work-Folk') and Auguste Comte who saw the social sciences as the culminating point of the work of the conventional sciences in a whole world-view. In other words, Geddes found in France the stirrings of a movement back towards a generalist and philosophical spirit in European thinking. And he made it his aim to further this by uniting the two approaches to the social sciences: the particular approach of Le Play and the general approach of Comte. From these heights he turned a radical, critical eye back on the culture from which he had sprung, castigating the conventional scientist as 'necrologist' rather than 'biologist', and declaring that 'the age of mechanical dualism is ending'. He called for a new way of looking at and living on the earth, looking forward to a 'geotechnical' world evolving from the 'neotechnics' and 'paleotechnics' of the previous two hundred years.

The proximity to White's vocabulary is evident – though the move from geo-technicality to geopoetics is a big one. Interestingly, Geddes' multi-disciplinary approach to human existence on the earth leads him also to an *aesthetic* conclusion which we see developed by Kenneth White. In Geddes' vision, the perceiver, and the expression perception stimulates, are back on board:

When we add up the aesthetic subfunctions of all

'necessary' ultimate products, and add to this the vast
quantity of purely aesthetic products, we see how small the
fundamental element of production has become in relation
to the superior, and reach the paradoxical generalisation
that production – though fundamentally for maintenance –
is mainly for 'art'.[4]

It was Patrick Geddes who coined the term 'the Scottish
Renaissance' which was taken up by Hugh MacDiarmid for
whom Geddes was a major influence, and applied it to the rather
dismal cultural-intellectual scene of early twentieth century
Scotland.

For George Davie, the latter stages of the Democratic
Intellect, which he describes in *The Crisis of the Democratic
Intellect*[5], were characterised by Masson's injunction to
'internalise' the distinctive Scottish elements in what he was
prepared to accept as a British culture. The Scottish influence
(which he recognised and favoured) would best be continued not
by overt advocacy and expression, rather by quiet participation
in British society, allowing the distinctive Scottish contribution
to come through, as it were, on its own. MacDiarmid attempted
to break this compliance with the British project by reopening
the intellectual current in Scottish life, starting himself from a
thorough and wide reading in the French poetic tradition of
Laforgue, Valéry etc., and by consciously adopting a 'synthetic'
Scots language in which to express himself.

In philosophical terms, MacDiarmid's move was all about
perception. According to George Davie, in his long study of
Hugh MacDiarmid in *The Crisis*, new, clearer vision can only be
achieved through an aggressive challenge to the routine,

accustomed modes of perception. People do not see what is really there, but see what they are encouraged to see unless and until someone or something forces them to look differently, from a new angle, with new linguistic apparatus. This is the function of MacDiarmid's synthetic Scots – it stops people thinking that 'it goes without saying' and forces them to pay attention in a new way to the world, perception of which had become deadened by 'a heavily technical and traditional vocabulary which weakened and hid the life in ideas'. That this has been translated, post-MacDiarmid, into a Scots language renaissance has done much to obscure the real aim of MacDiarmid's poetics. But MacDiarmid went far beyond this concern with perception and its implications for poetic technique and language. He also focussed attention on the content of poetics: the volcano he ignited (and personified), spat out material from all over the world, from disciplines and cultures, minority and majority, across the globe and across time – ideas such as had never been considered as part of mainstream culture before, except of course on the continent to which the Scots had been increasingly struggling to remain connected. He undertook, by himself, a massive shifting of Scottish cultural-intellectual perspectives which many of his compatriots are still trying to focus, and which some, consciously or unconsciously, obfuscate and reduce to their own conceptions.

The closeness of White to Buchanan hardly needs to be insisted on. It is there at the biographical level: the constant connection with France, teaching at the Sorbonne, the long stay in the south-west. It is there at the poetic-literary level, with poetry rising into cosmology.

A similar biographical parallel can be drawn with Geddes, in the general attraction to the French intellectual field, and in the fact that White's place in Brittany is only a few miles from the sea-town, Roscoff, where Geddes did his early boundary-breaking studies in biology. But the parallel goes far beyond this coincidental level. It is there in the philosophical and scientific criticism of science as 'paleotechnics', and in the attempt to open a more radical and more general field.

But it is maybe with MacDiarmid that a comparison is most illuminating – MacDiarmid the writer trying to bring back the energies of the Renaissance. White is close to MacDiarmid in many ways. He shares the same scope, the same wide range of materials as MacDiarmid, while trying to give it all, by selection, more concentrated form, and more natural rhythm. But it is in the far intellectual perspectives that White and MacDiarmid are specially close, whereas most writing done elsewhere, whether in English, Scots or Gaelic is nowhere near them, has no conception of them. The difference here is that MacDiarmid is often content to *refer* to these higher reaches, to put them on the map, whereas White has gone further into their territory to work on them.

One of the many links between MacDiarmid and White is assuredly MacDiarmid's great poem 'On a Raised Beach':

> *What happens to us*
> *Is irrelevant to the world's geology*
> *But what happens to the world's geology*
> *Is not irrelevant to us.*
> *We must reconcile ourselves to the stones,*
> *Not the stones to us.*
> *Here a man must shed the encumbrances that muffle*

Contact with elemental things, the subtleties
That seem inseparable from a humane life, and go apart
Into a simple and sterner, more beautiful and more
oppressive world,
Austerely intoxicating: the first draught is overpowering;
Few survive it.[6]

This is exactly what White did. From early on, he much frequented those 'raised beaches' of perception and conceptions, and he has tried to work out a semantics and language that, in the words of William Carlos Williams (one of the American poets to whom White is close), will 'reconcile the people and the stones'.

The big difference between MacDiarmid and White, of course, is that MacDiarmid stayed stubbornly in Scotland, while White (like Joyce with Ireland), felt the need at one point to get out and away. Much of this difference can and no doubt will be made of both by genuine Nationalists and by those looking for any excuse to set aside a work that perturbs their complacence. But a closer acquaintance with the life of the man C. M. Grieve, who lay behind the arch-nationalist pseudonym of MacDiarmid, shows that his existence was far from devoid of internal tension and contradiction. And a close reading of the poems, not stopping at *A Drunk Man Looking at the Thistle* or the *Hymns to Lenin*, will reveal passages pointing directly to White's choice and trajectory, as in, for example, the *Letter to R. M. B.*:

Nae man, nae spiritual force, can live
In Scotland lang. For God's sakes leave it tae
Mak a warld o' your ain.[7]

White's main motivation was to find a context more propitious than the British one for the literary, poetic and intellectual work he wanted to pursue. But he left taking a lot of Scotland with him, and with the idea of coming back, either in person or via opus, perhaps both. While working away on his own, he was moving more and more towards a world open to all.

2. Universal Ancestor: The Shaman

In his move to go farther and further back, into primalness (a move which started with his going 'up the back' in Fairlie), White came at one time on the figure common to both West and East (as to North and South) of the shaman. Traces of him appear here and there, again and again, in White's writing, be it essay ('A Shaman Dancing on the Glacier'[8]), prose narrative (*The Blue Road*[9]), or poem ('The Shaman's Way'[10]).

In addition to his reading in the 'exact' sciences, White from early on did a great deal of reading in anthropology and ethnology. The great texts of anthropology-ethnology-ethnography: Franz Boas' *Kwakiutl Ethnography*, Malinowski's *Argonauts of the Western Pacific*, Lévi-Strauss' *Sad Tropics* are familiar territory to him. But no text probably gave his mind such a jolt as Mircea Eliade's, *Shamanism and the Archaic Techniques of Ecstasy*, which he found in Paris.

Here's what White has to say about the encounter in the aforementioned essay, 'A Shaman Dancing on the Glacier':

As I read through that book, I came across more and more correspondences between what he was laying out and my own early experience. In other words, I realised I had stumbled on to shamanism, had practised a kind of home-made shamanism, that is, an immemorial tradition going back to neolithic, paleolithic and prelithic times, elements of which can be found all over the world, from Siberia to Australia via the Americas and Oceania. This isn't really as surprising as it may sound. It's almost certain that, given enough scope, enough freedom, a child will go through all the past phases of humanity, from fishes to philosophers.

And he goes on to give concrete examples of those correspondences between his own early practices on the shores, in the woods, and on the moors of Fairlie and traditional shamanism, such as, for example, the fascination for crystal and quartz, the attraction to trees and birds and various rituals (standing under waterfalls, etc.).

In the essay 'A Shaman Dancing on the Glacier', he has this to say:

What I suggest is that shamanism began when man began moving over the earth after the retreat of the last glacier. He is on the hunt for animals, but it is with reverence, and he has great awe of the glacier, remains of which still lie up there on the heights – the original 'white goddess'?[11]

Thereafter (for example, in the poem 'The Master of the Labyrinth'[12], written after frequent visits to the paleolithic painted caves of south-west France and north-west Spain), White traces the path of the shaman through different contexts and cultures.

The first plastic manifestation of the shaman is in the bird-man figure in the Lascaux caves which was painted about 25,000 years ago. In the period before that, from about 50,000 years before our era, we find bone remains which appear to be ritual offerings and have been related by experts to the archaic idea of animals returning to life from their bones – an idea whose presence is echoed in the symbolism and ecstatic techniques of the shaman who dreams of his skeleton, who decorates himself with bones, who plays his drum with a bone – bones of his familiar birds and animals with whom he is one.

Moving nearer in space and time, there is the Germanic god Odin, who spent nine days and nights hanging in a tree in order to learn the sacred runes. His two companions are crows called Thought and Memory. The Odinic myth is of clear shamanic structure.

Among the Celts we have the god Curnunnos pictured on the Gundestrup cauldron of 100 BC. He sits in yogic posture, has antlers on his head and is surrounded by totemic animals: deer, bear, wolf. In the key Celtic lore surrounding the figure of Finn and the Fiannadh, his sons Oscar and Ossian have names related to the deer. The Fiannadh also had shamanistic attributes: they had to be of excellent physical prowess, they had to leave family and clan behind them, and they had to know 'the twelve essential books of poetry'. It could well be that this poetic knowledge was what Irish scholars came to Scotland to learn from Pictish druids who, as White has noted in an essay in *La Figure du dehors*[13], are described in an old Gaelic text as wearing animal hides on their bodies and bird feathers in their hair.

Another obstinate survival of a shamanist element in this part of the world can be seen in a series of poems dating from the thirteenth century through to the present day. In 'Thomas The Rhymer', as White has argued in various publications[14], what might appear 'strange' elements belong to the archaic world-view. 'True Thomas', as he is known, is seen first in relation to mountain (Eildon Hills) and tree – centres of the world. Here he is met by the Queen of Faerie who takes Thomas away from the Earth on a journey to 'elfinland'. This 'fayre ladye' is, of course, Graves' 'white goddess', the Greeks' Muse, or, in the Celtic Tradition, the Cailleach, the old woman, or her lovely daughter whose presence is reflected in the names of so many Scottish mountains. After seven years, Thomas returns with the gifts of poetry – 'the tongue which can never lee' – and 'sight'. In the thirteenth century version which we have, a Christian element has, of course, crept in, but it has not overcome the archaic tradition which the ballad retains. In the Ballad, 'Tam Linn', there are stronger hints of the idea of a Christian tradition overcoming the old tradition, but it is that shamanistic tradition which continues to provide the authentic narrative and poetic power in the ballad as Tam is turned into various animals – a snake, a dog, a toad – before being turned back into 'a mother-naked man' in his journey back from the Queen of Elfinland's realm. In the context of these two ballads, Robert Burns' tale of 'Tam O' Shanter' begins to deepen its connotations while revealing a narrowing of perception and experience. As White demonstrates in an essay in *On Scottish Ground*, the shamanistic echoes in 'Tam O' Shanter' are strong but what is overcoming them here is a weakness, a loss of energy – that of eighteenth century Rationalism. Tam o' Shanter is the man of rationalist-humanist modernity who, in his drunkenness, has a vision of the world of the Cailleach and her lovely daughter but is too afraid to follow them and runs away to rediscover domesticity, chased by those who are represented in the modern context by the word 'witches'. A poem which has been generally considered as 'a piece of comic realism, humorous and exuberant, an extravagant fantasy', is interpreted by White as the image of the modern dilemma – withdrawal into the supposedly safe parameters of the personal-social context (work, family, church and common sense) relieved by alcohol to regain that 'sense of world', caricatured here, as a larger world, elsewhere by images of witchcraft, ghosts, monsters – all the fantasia that's left when the real ground is gone.

Here we arrive at the strictly contemporary situation, marked by more or less numb and comfortable, more or less vicious and violent nihilism and with a cultural need, not just for more cultural products, but for a practice as deep and powerful as shamanism.

We begin, a minority radically, the majority timidly and tentatively, to recognise our neglected and abused earth as our fundamental ground of being. And from this new ground can develop new ways of thinking and being, and the need for a new language adequate to the expression of this new cultural outlook.

This is more than the 'alternatives' or the 'revolutions' we have heard so much about. The immense impact of industrialism, accompanied by the consequent narrow sense of history which dominates our educational curriculum, has encouraged us to see alternatives to the Western established tradition in revolutionary political movements. Although the visions of many Western revolutionaries were, initially, profound and far-reaching, the struggle with the established line saw them subsumed into it. There is little of real substance to distinguish ('reactionary') religious faith from ('progressive') political faith. Whatever their stated aims, and Christianity has been quick to adopt the language of the Left in the post-war era, what makes both 'reactionary' is to be found in the word 'faith' which roots both in the idealist foundations of the West. Faith cannot change the West because the West *is* 'faith'. Similarly, if we move from 'faith' to the more fertile concept, 'knowledge', unless we free our thinking from the notion that the categorising analytical approach laid down by Aristotle is adequate to *all* conceptual and perceptual contexts, then we will continue to fail to see the world as it is. For certain purposes, it is useful to hold that one thing cannot be another, but how *truly* meaningful is it to hold that, for example, earth and flower (and air, and light, and rain . . .) are separate things? To use a more abstract language, if it is necessary to see the many, it is necessary also to see the one, to grasp the whole.

What ultimately interests White in the shaman is that here we have a figure with a poetic-therapeutic role in society whose practice goes away beyond the role of 'the artist' in modern society: reflector of the state of things (hand-maid to the sociologist), representative of 'culture', upholder of 'aesthetic values', provider of fantasia, etc., etc. The shaman has a larger role. Whereas all those figures just evoked act and exhibit within the socio-human context, the shaman maintains the contact open between the socio-human context and the world, the universe at large. While concentrating all the psychic and cultural energies of the social group (tribe), he is also the great outsider, which is to say the great whole-holder.

This is where shamanism, abstracted, enters into, flows into geopoetics.

In the Introduction to *Le Plateau de l'albatros*, White offers this description of the geopoetic field:

> . . . one could say that it concerns a new mental cartography, a conception of life disengaged at last from ideologies, myths, religions etc., and the search for a language capable of expressing this other way of being in the world, but making it clear from the start that this is a question of a rapport with the earth (energies, rhythms, forms) not a subjugation to Nature. I'm talking about the search (from place to place, step by step) for a poetics situated, or, rather, moving outside the established systems of representation. Discourse in movement, then, rather than emphatic denunciation or infinite deconstruction. But this is only a preliminary outline. The accent here is not on definition, but on desire, a desire for life and for world [. . .]. It is about a *movement* which concerns the very manner in which man grounds his existence on earth.[15]

Before going further into the field of geopoetics, let's try and sum up the shaman's way in its relevance to that field.

Firstly, the shaman's identifying technique of ecstasy presents him as an original artist figure. The poet or artist also 'stands (or moves) outside' the personal-social context to penetrate deep into the territory of perception, deep into participation in the earth. Like Brandan in the prow of his ship at the end of White's poem 'Brandan's Last Voyage'[16], the poet-artist sails off 'into the white unknown', but with the intention of writing down what he finds. He is a seeker (an informed seeker – he has had his didactic as well as his ecstatic experience) after the ultimate experience, the ultimate perception, with a desire to arrive at a *composition* of those experiences and perceptions, not just for its own sake, but in order to offer them back to the community.

According to Kenneth White, in modernity this image of the artist is nowhere to be seen. It was only to be expected that modernity's plunge into rationalism and humanism be expressed in a 'novel' form of literature – fiction – which focusses on a narrower and shallower field than had any literature up to that point. In modernity the artist no longer knows the ecstatic techniques of his ancient avatar. He has become the documentarist of society – he mopes around inside the closed circle taking notes here, commenting there, smiling wryly then, weeping sentimentally now, as disinclined to go beyond the city walls (or the estate's fences) as any puritan goodman of New England was to enter the forest of the 'savage'. Then modernity's artist, despairing of the tedious formalities of Augustan verse and the shallow gossip of the novel, hears again the call of something wilder in the background and ventures out into Romanticism. Soon, though, he ends up sighing, seeing nothing in the world any more but never-ending sequences of symbols. In the twentieth century we have seen the collapse of modernity's scientific and philosophical foundations and, where artists and writers have been alive to this, they have once again moved off into the outside to seek a bigger perceptual field.

Secondly, the shamanistic nature of art and poetry is underlined by the shaman's role as custodian of those archaic images and themes of the original cosmic perception. Throughout history (and the shaman is by his very nature pre-historic) it recurs in myths, legends, tales and, in its presence, when evoked in live authentic expression, we feel an inexplicable frisson of recognition as we find ourselves, via the shamanistic expression, tuning into his nostalgic evocation.

This is not an argument for a return to myth, folklore, religion etc. as White is careful to emphasise in the extract from *Le Plateau de l'albatros* quoted at the beginning of this section. That was the step taken by Romanticism, the first great movement back to a desire for participation in the earth. In many ways this was inevitable because Romanticism was a movement in reaction against industrialised modernity and because it discovered its sense of other dimensions in folklore, the study of which at the time was intricately connected with nationalist movements. In this political context the insights to be gained in folklore were, inevitably, narrower and shallower than a wider context would allow. The consequences in certain areas were disastrous and, as White points out in his essay[17], it has been peculiarly difficult to approach Nordic mythology in particular ever since. Today, while not suggesting that any nefarious intention is involved (fascism, though, breeds on naivety), similar returns to mythology and religions are evident in reaction to the environmental crisis, and the shaman has been a strong focus of interest for many of these movements. For White, geopoetics, as a set of ideas and practices, and as an 'Institute', is necessary to give a more rigorous and clear analysis and expression of our current situation and to provide the movement with a forward impetus. Geopoetics seeks to move with these far-reaching areas of the sciences and the philosophies to bring them together and to seek the language they require to compose themselves into coherent, authentic expression.

Thirdly, there is the linguistic question, the search for what White calls 'a language psychologically deep, aesthetically charged and, if possible, socio-logically effective'[18]. One of the most striking features of the shaman's ecstasy is the language which he develops to speak his penetrating vision. Eliade tells us that the Yakut shaman's poetic vocabulary is twelve thousand words strong, compared to four thousand in the language of his community. In his conclusion to *Shamanism: The Archaic Techniques of Ecstasy*, he proposes that the two great strains of poetry as they developed in the West – epic and lyric – originate in the shaman's ecstasy: the shaman's song of his great journeys provides the subjects, motifs, characters and images of epic poetry; and, in the pre-ecstatic euphoria of the shaman, lies the universal source of lyric poetry. The shaman's drumming takes him to a 'second state' wherein linguistic creation and the rhythms of lyric poetry are to be found.

In the early twentieth century, Wallace Stevens summed up the situation facing the artist with a statement which is one of Kenneth White's starting points for geopoetics – 'the great poems of Heaven and Hell have been written; it remains to write the poem of the earth'[19]. The language of such a poem would have to be spontaneous, 'natural', like the shaman's. Poetic ecstasy is 'natural', the 'normal' condition of man is artificial, as is his language. When we are so far into the perception of things as to have grasped their essence, says Edmund Husserl, founder of transcendental phenomenology, our expression will be 'poetic', in all other instances we merely 'opine'. The focus of the poet's attention, then, is, primarily, not on (artificial) form, but on that point at which essential perception of the world (in micro- or macro-cosm), so truly felt as to necessitate its being expressed, meets its form in its emergence into being (its voicing). Among the shamans of the Americas (who reached there by crossing the Bering Straits or by sailing the Pacific from the Northern and Central Asian territories), their function, as well as those already described, was to recount the tale of the migration, which they do, so as to evoke the deep memories of the people. In European North America of the nineteenth century, Henry David Thoreau constantly finds himself, in *Walden*, contemplating the nature of expression as a result of experiencing the expression of nature, in some of the most beautiful moments in that beautiful book. Talking about an owl hooting, he calls it, 'such a sound as the frozen earth would yield if struck with a suitable plectrum, the very lingua franca of Walden Wood'[20]. The poet's work, then, is to strike this earth-plectrum.

We are concerned, in shamanism as with White's intellectual nomadism and geopoetics, with a travelling, a vision and a language.

In the chapter 'A Short Introduction to Eskimo Studies' of *Incandescent Limbo*, White presents the shaman Atungai:

> Atungai was a great shaman and he wanted to go round the world [. . .]. So he set out. And soon came to a steep, high cliff. It's when he came to the steep, high cliff that he began in earnest his trip around the world. He was a great shaman, so he always kept to the margins. When he'd seen all the different peoples of the earth, he came back home. But he came home by a road different from the one he took on his way out. He was a really great shaman.[21]

It is hard not to see in this Eskimo account of a Netsilik

shaman set by White in his *Incandescent Limbo* a transposed account of White's own itinerary.

In his book, *Dreaming with Open Eyes – the Shamanic Spirit in Twentieth Century Art and Culture*, Michael Tucker places Kenneth White, along with Rainer Maria Rilke and Gunnar Ekelöf, as among 'the greatest shamans of twentieth-century poetry'[22].

3. Cultural Analysis Now

If most literature is content simply to mirror society (placing a story in this or that social context, or adding diverse fantastical, phantasmal layers to it), what lies at the basis of White's writing and thinking activity, in addition to a mass of basic experience, is a radical culture-analysis.

At the psychological level, this began in Glasgow, with his reading of Freud (*Civilisation and its Discontents*) and Ferenczi (*Thalassa – Psychoanalysis of the Origins of Sexual Life*). It was continued later in France, with his reading of Herbert Marcuse's *Eros and Civilisation*, and, later again, when already well grounded in White's mind, it came in touch with the schizo-analytic cartography of Guattari and Deleuze, in, for example, the *Anti-Oedipus*.

On the socio-historical level, Glasgow itself was a text.

White inherited a lot from Glasgow: a grotesque, often black humour raised into a philosophical supernihilism. More objectively, he saw in the city a paradigm of modern, or late-modern, civilisation. It was Gerard Manley Hopkins (an early influence, it will be remembered, on White), employed as a preacher in the city for some time, who said that one look at Glasgow was enough to make you have grave doubts about civilisation. What White saw in Glasgow was modernity in its death throes. While being well aware, of course, of the Gaelic origin of the name ('the green place'), he amused himself, in Lacanian fashion, by interpreting the name of his native town as *glas* (French for 'knell', a death signal), and *go* (in other words: get the hell out).

As a student, White had read also Jung's *Modern Man in Search of a Soul*. He liked neither the book nor its vocabulary (he did not see himself at all as looking for 'a soul'). But he found it symptomatic. And it was one of the books that set him to thinking if there might be the possibility of an anthropological figure different from Modern Man, who was, largely, citified man.

It's here that White's culture-analysis turned into cultural revolution.

During his first sojourn in Paris, when he was plunged in Surrealism, working at a thesis on the relationship between poetry and politics, White was studying all the deviant cultural movements that Europe had known, from the Brethren of the Free Spirit of the Middle Ages up to clandestine groups such as The White Dove of pre-revolutionary Russia. He was deeply absorbed in synthesising historical texts, such as Spengler's *Decline of the West*, which he summed up in the following manner:

> . . . (Western) culture had spent its forces and was now
> entering its final state of civilisation: it was dying, as other
> cultures – Indian, Babylonian, Chinese, Egyptian, Arabian,
> Mexican – had lived and died.[23]

Spengler's vision of the whole process of history – 'a huge historico-cultural prose-poem' says White – fascinated him. In Spengler, he found the figure of what he would call 'the intellectual nomad'. This is the independent thinker, the individualist intellectual, operating outside the institutions and categories of civilisation, pursuing his own paths of experience but, by signs and interventions here and there, communicating his thoughts back into the communities from which he is estranged. In Spengler's case, however, the intellectual nomad remains within the city walls. What White was looking for, a desire springing from his experiences on the Western seaboard, was

> the possibility of a renewed contact with the landscape,
> and maybe the elaboration of a new mindscape. That's what
> I had in mind when I used to cross the Clyde by the
> Whiteinch Ferry and walk the thirty odd miles down the
> coast to Fairlie.[24]

Toynbee's *A Study of History* was also a key reference in those days. Here White particularly related to the dialogue between liberalism and communism viewed by Toynbee not so much as an economic-political question regarding the self-sacrificing collective as opposed to exploitative personal enterprise, but more as a cultural question – the right to intellectual freedom. For Toynbee, this right was rooted in Christianity and, contrary to Spengler's fatalism, he seeks a religious regeneration of Western culture. As White points out, Toynbee was not alone in this. T. S. Eliot gave poetic voice to Spengler's fatalistic vision in 'The Waste Land' and then reverted to Anglican Christianity and political conservatism. Similarly, in the aftermath of the downfall of the Stalinist regimes of Eastern Europe there is evidence of a return to orthodox religion. White takes no interest in such religious revivalism.

Coming from a socialist background, he retained for a while some attachment to the possibilities inherent in Communism as he felt that Communism at least had 'a project', but moved farther and farther away from it:

> In Glasgow I read Plekhanov's 'Essay on the Development of the Monist Conception of History', and later on, in Paris, I read one after the other of the marxist and communist texts put out by the Moscow Editions, but more and more out of a sense of duty and solidarity than with any real conviction (the philosophical judgements of the communist dictionaries and encyclopaedias were abominably simplistic) – it was only after May 1968 that I abandoned this line entirely.[25]

In his study of the phalansterist, Charles Fourier[26], White is clearly attracted by his vision of 'Harmony'. But socialism had hardly followed that large vision:

> Not only has the word lost its force, so that even the most sordid of politicians can let it cross their lips, but the movement has silted up in compromise and third-rate manoeuvring, and the idea died for lack of moral and intellectual fire, with only lone individuals or the smallest of groups to keep it alive.

The itinerary White was to embark on was already taking shape in the failure of the political alternative – an itinerary which, while no longer engaging in naive optimism, will have nothing to do with its even more life-destroying corollary, resigned pessimism:

> There is no room any more for an easy optimism (even Whitman, when he came to write *Democratic Vistas*, was less optimistic than when he started out). On the other hand, I think it is impossible to give way to a resigned pessimism (if there is to be pessimism, at least let it be Nietzschean-Dionysiac). There may still be enough fluctuant life-energy and moral-intellectual fire around to make for a new revolutionary climate, one that will not express itself perhaps by a sudden upheaval, but by a quiet underground movement, by growth rather than revolt.

It was with this knowledge and those ideas in his head that he came back to Glasgow, started up the Jargon Group, and began to print off a series of pamphlets, called the *Jargon Papers*.

The Jargon Group took the form of seminars and readings in topics and authors not usually found in the established curricula. One participant, Norman Bissell, describes it:

> It was the only place for miles around where you could get Whitman and Nietzsche, with Japanese haiku, Chinese Taoism, anarchism and deviant communism coming at you week in and week out, all presented in White's particular style: fast thinking and bright image-filled talk.[27]

The underlying critique upon which White's activities were (and continue to be) based, had political inspirations and implications, but the focus was very much on the culture question. He analyses and criticises not only the 'abject cynicism' of the 'dispensers' of trash demagogically called 'popular' (for White a people can be culturally demanding, and democracy ought to be demanding), but also a more dynamic conception of culture:

> What is this conception of culture that prevails in our society? It is the objective conception, which sees culture as something separate from the men who make it, which sees it as an *object to be acquired*, and to be dispensed.[28]

There is a sense of the 'end of an era' about the Jargon Papers and activities, an impatient, energetic style which recalls Nietzsche in *Thus Spoke Zarathustra* and looks with urgency towards a new beginning:

> Life, instead of being the deep, intense, lovely experience, the experience of wholeness it can be, becomes divided: on the one hand a sophisticated and polite inanity, on the other loutish vulgarity and violence; on the one hand empty intellectualism, on the other morbid fantasies. Wherever the full nature of man is not realised, there will be dualisms of this kind. It is when these dualisms reach extreme points that the end of an era comes. That is what is happening today.[29]

There was another man saying things similar to what White was saying, and that was Alexander Trocchi, himself a Glaswegian, who had left Glasgow first for France then for California, before coming back to Britain via London, where he set up the Sigma Project, which was a plan to create a worldwide network of minds engaged in ideas of cultural revolution through the distribution of roneotyped texts (R. D. Laing, another Glaswegian was also part of this). It was not inevitable that the two should meet, but it was appropriate. The first move came from Trocchi, who, after seeing the early Jargon Papers and pieces by White in magazines, wrote to him, inviting him to come in on the Project in any way he liked. White did indeed contribute to the Sigma Portfolio, and the Jargon Papers, which White and members of the Jargon Group had simply distributed by hand in the streets of Glasgow, were relayed further afield by Trocchi's organisation.

The two finally met, in London. But if White definitely felt affinities with Trocchi on the intellectual level, his attitude to Trocchi's life-context was one of amused distance. He offers a caricatural presentation of his meeting with Trocchi in the first chapter of *Travels in the Drifting Dawn*, 'London Underground', where the seriousness and validity of the project are underlined in relating it to similar 'underground' cultural movements from history, but are seen as undermined by the pathetic, dope-centred context in which the participants are living. White later commented:

> I liked Trocchi, he had a good mind and he could write. But it was a lousy context he'd got himself into, and he was up to his neck in it.[30]

In a booklet[31] which otherwise suffers from several errors of fact and judgement, Gavin Bowd points out that while Trocchi was still in a humanist context, White's impetus is 'post-humanist' and it has led him to the formulation of geopoetics, the possibility of answers to the existential and cultural problems he, like Trocchi, had identified, but which the latter could not formulate successfully. As White puts it in *Incandescent Limbo*, in a turn of phrase which he will use in other contexts too:

Not the underground, another ground.[32]

During those four years in Glasgow, while his own thought was advancing on all fronts, White was more and more conscious of a 'circumscribed context', both inside the university and outside it, and lived with an increasing sense of isolation.

He got relief from the situation by writing, in his back room off Great Western Road, what he called 'long, scrawling manuscripts' filled with *alter ego* characters called 'Mungo Reilly, Logan the Loner or Archie Pelago'. But these he conceived of as therapeutic-work, like some kind of automatic writing, and he never considered publishing them.

He was beginning to feel that, for the moment, he had 'done his bit' in Scotland, and that to pursue his life and work he would have to go elsewhere. To continue at the university as it was would be to exist more and more like a bear in a cage. As for the Jargon Group, he sensed that it had reached its limits. And there was no sense in wandering forever about Glasgow.

His state of mind at the time is summed up in the poem 'Crow Meditation Text':

> *I once thought of founding*
> *an Academy of Gulls*
> *(based on an ancient*
> *Chinese model)*

with one aim in view:
dawn-talk
grammar of rain, tree, stone
blood and bone

[...]

but that plan went with the wind
and I ended up
with broken wings
on a cold island

smoking the weeds of my mind. [33]

He was going to continue to work in universities. He was going to continue founding 'gull academies'. But he needed, for the moment, another context.

Which is why he decided to leave again for France where, for a start, he was involved in the revolt of '68.

4. The Drifting Dawn

White took up a post as lecturer in English at the University of Pau in the Atlantic Pyrenees Departement in the south-west of France in the autumn of 1967. As somebody already known of as 'a poet', he was viewed with some suspicion from the start, a suspicion justified by his immediate involvement in extra-curricular activities. As he had done with the Jargon Group in

Glasgow, he now organised a group in Pau which produced the review *Feuillage*, its name a deliberate reference to Whitman's 'leaves' ('always our old feuillage . . . always the free range and diversity'[34]). Its first editorial made clear its radical ground stating that, although *Feuillage* was coming out of a university, 'what we are immediately concerned with is a *living university* – not a mere diploma-factory'[35]. It is clear from this and his approach to university teaching and learning in Glasgow in previous years, that White had already come to the conclusions about educational and general culture which were to bring French students out onto the streets in the 'events' of May '68.

White was with the students, recognising a desire for cultural revolution in the movement, but he began to take his distance as it became in his eyes harnessed to simplistic political motivations, losing its larger perspectives. 'Not Mao, the Tao!' was one of his slogans.

In White's eyes society was not yet ready for the deep cultural as opposed to political revolution that he had long ago concluded was necessary. He sums up his attitude to May '68 in *The Blue Road*:

> . . . a good many people in France at that time wanted to see the end of a certain culture and were feeling out the beginnings of something else. That *'something else'* has still to be discovered, but it seems to me that it will mean among other things a move from history to geography.[36]

With this in mind, he abandoned the Marxist line which he had studied widely but 'more out of a sense of duty and solidarity than with any real conviction'[37] and plunged himself into a deep and extensive study of geology, geomorphology, and all kinds of geographical texts, including old travel books. He had the time to do so now because his involvement in the May events gave the university authorities the excuse they needed to sack him.

The year 1968 also saw what was to be the last of his books to be published in English for twenty years, that collection of poems entitled *The Most Difficult Area* (Cape, 1968) – apart from two volumes of translation from André Breton: *Selected Poems* and *Ode to Charles Fourier* which were both published in 1969. He was, then, truly isolated and, although he took up a post of 'lecteur' in Paris in 1969, and founded another review, *The Feathered Egg*, again involving his students in a publication pursuing the idea of cultural revolution, this took up relatively little of his time, and after a year in Paris (working at the final composition of *Incandescent Limbo*), he remained based in Pau:

> From my study window, I could see a great length of the Pyrenean chain, in front of me the Pic du Midi d'Ossau, the last great granite peak before the chain tails off to the West, towards the Pic d'Anie, on the edge of the Basque country, the Mont Orhy and La Rhune.[38]

There he continued and extended his studies in philosophy, the sciences, anthropology, languages and literature and wrote poetry, essays and prose with little attempt at publication beyond the occasional piece in a review.

It was from Pau that he began a series of journeys round the ports of Europe and then to Asia and North America, many of which journeys provided the material for his prose-narrative books beginning with *Travels in the Drifting Dawn*.

If White's geopoetics are fundamentally based on raised beaches (areas of expanded consciousness), he neglects none of the intervening stages, and all of them are represented in the 'waybooks' he began writing at this time. Among those intervening stages lies the phenomenon of the city, which stands at the beginning of civilisation as we know it.

Cities (in White's experience: Munich, Paris, Amsterdam, Hong Kong, Bangkok, Tokyo, Montreal . . .) are dotted all along his itineraries. His waybooks usually start in one of them before moving out onto uncongested roads and paths. If they are the hives, sometimes the hell-holes, of modernity, marked, except for some quiet areas and moments, by confusion, incoherence, cacophony, they are always portrayed with sympathy, the sometimes ferocious satire is often accompanied by a gentle kind of humour, and there is never a complacency in the immediate sordidness, on the contrary, an attempt is always made to open out a larger perspective.

Here's a return to Glasgow:

> Coming into Glasgow again. The mauve evening thickening into purple above the orange-lighted streets. A drunk bleeding in a close. A woman's voice on Exchange Square: 'She had a bad time wi yon bastard.' 'Late final, late final.'[39]

Here is Barcelona:

> . . . away at the dead end of the Calle San Pablo, where there are no longer any women visible, only men humped in sordid drink-shops with pale blue TV screens flickering in the darkness, yes, this is the end, with a pale-green-painted

little hospital-looking shop there advertising *lavajes-siphilis*,
the syphilitic end of the overhuman bloody world.[40]

The scene is full of signs of a civilisation at its end – the
'dead-end' street, echoing the 'late final' of the Glasgow image,
is that of St. Paul, establisher of Christian orthodoxy, the
'darkness' in which the TV screens flicker is a cultural and
intellectual darkness. The human hopelessness of it recalls the
extreme negativist E. M. Cioran's dark definition of
contemporary man in his *A Short History of Decomposition*: 'a
convalescent aspiring to disease'[41]. Modern man, according to
Cioran, 'no longer lives in existence, but in the theory of
existence'. In a telling phrase, he claims that modern alienated
man 'lives in order to unlearn ecstasy'.

In his essays[42], which range with great erudition and acute
intelligence over the cultural map, White casts a critical eye
upon the two main attempts which have been made to deal with
the existential problem outlined here – the political method of
Marxism and the psychoanalytical method originating with
Freud. Close to European critics such as, among others, Gilles
Deleuze and Félix Guattari, notably in *L'Anti-Œdipe* (Anti-
Oedipus), and Jean-François Lyotard in *Dérive à partir de Marx et
Freud*, he indicates that psycho-analysis (whatever the rare
insights of, say, an R. D. Laing or a Wilhelm Reich) has, as its
main function, the repatriation of the sick spirit back into the
alien land which made it sick in the first place, to get the
disaffected child back into the (disaffecting) family as a
functioning member. It is becoming clearer too, that political
movements, as we have known them up to now, offer no genuine
path out of the malaise. This is not summarily nor totally to

dismiss psycho-analysis and politics – we live in the modern world and they have their function. But they do not go far enough beyond the palliative, and what White proposes is a larger field of thought and action, a truly radical analysis of our situation which, according to him, requires a larger perspective and a deeper penetration into the nature of being and the world.

In artistic terms, he is coming to the conclusion that even radical writers such as Samuel Beckett stay within the parameters of the received description of civilisation:

> The whole of Western civilisation is a compound of expectations whether it be for the Messiah, the Future or God knows what. Even when it's given up waiting for anything else, doesn't it keep waiting for Godot?[43]

Samuel Beckett's expression for the state of civilisation is 'endgame'. For White, Beckett pushes the boundaries of nihilism further and further out, while White himself seeks to take the step across those boundaries:

> I'm ready to go far along Samuel Beckett's road, as far as he'll go, right to the end. But that's it: Samuel Beckett is at the end of something . . . and all the time he's pushing the end a little further out, infinite calculation of despair pushed as far as a perfect non-art, but he never makes the jump, never goes *beyond the end*, he marks time at that spot, and he marks time better than anyone. But I feel myself beyond endgame.[44]

The movement beyond nihilism cannot be a collective movement as commonly understood. Rather it is anarchist in nature, to be undertaken by individuals whose influence may then spread, stimulating other individuals so that numbers multiply and, perhaps, eventually, a movement might arise, which could revolutionise society not from a standpoint under a banner (this is always exploited by a power group or a class) but on the basis of knowledge and awareness – individuals sharing a grounding, living a shared culture of perception as opposed to an imposed culture of *faith* (be that faith political or religious). The image of the movement sought here by White is not of monolithic, one-directional movement, rather it is archipelagical ('The archipelagical as against the institutional'[45]).

The American poet, Gary Snyder, working out of the American context, puts the initial impetus to this more radical questioning in this way:

> I thought it was only capitalism that went wrong. Then I got into American Indian studies and I began to perceive that maybe it was all of Western culture that was off the track and not just capitalism – that there were certain self-destructive tendencies in our cultural tradition.[46]

White would associate himself with this, but not with Snyder's solution which is a religious one, the practice of Buddhism. Here, Snyder is expressing a desire for freedom from a narrowness of perspective which arises, partly, from the huge impact of industrialisation on the West at the beginning of the nineteenth century. You would have to go a long way back in history to find a change in human existence as enormous and sudden as that. It has shaped our view of the world; in a sense we date ourselves from that event. Now, the twentieth century has seen developments which invite a much larger view of time. Kenneth White, and others who work in this larger perspective, want to enter a fuller sense of time – into the points where time becomes space, into a *cosmological* perspective. This is about pushing back the boundaries of the personal, the social, the historical. Politics is not enough. The method required is, as we've seen, what White calls 'culture analysis'.

In a pamphlet put forward as a 'little cultural programme'[47], Kenneth White offers three definitions of 'culture'. The first concerns individual culture: 'the manner in which the human being conceives him/herself, works on him/herself, heads out towards a horizon'. That is, 'a conception of existence, a work-process . . . and some notion of the acme of human achievement.' The second deals with the social culture shared by a community: 'ensembles of motifs and motivations'. For example, in the Middle Ages everyone from peasant to philosopher to prince relates to the image of the Madonna and divine child. The third is the confused, degraded state in which we live: 'a bit of this and a bit of that [. . .] scraps of Christianity, bits of Greek Humanism, a little science, a drop of the exotic', the kind of thing which Nietzsche described as 'not fit for dogs'. Summing up the present situation, White says:

> In the strict sense of the word, we do not have a culture at all, except in the merely sociological sense (where 'culture' means football, bingo and the daily paper). What we do have is a mass of cultural (most often pseudo-cultural) production, in which you can find the best (but you need to have good eyesight), and the worst, but mostly great wads of mediocrity, what Paracelsus called a *cagastrum*, defended ideologically for its very mediocrity, which turns it

into mediocracy, the biggest political power there is. Under this kind of culture, the world is lost, world-lines are forgotten.[48]

For White, the awareness of this 'loss of world' was counterbalanced in his own, personal context, by the 'sense of world' he experienced, first on the Fairlie moors, later in similar places. The attempt to arrive at a coherent, and cohering, perspective from all these experiences was what exercised his mind most, created for him what he calls 'the fundamental cultural question' which centred on the possibilities for renewal and expansion of a 'sense of world'.

5. Radical European Thought

From now on, White would be moving in the larger context of Europe.

And what, radically considered, is Europe?

Nietzsche, Husserl and Heidegger see the point of departure for cultural Europe in Socratic philosophy. This is the point at which Europe breaks with Asia. This is the moment when, in Greece, the philosophical spirit of Reason is born. Europe, now the 'West', is the place born of philosophy, and the philosophy is metaphysical, based on a separation of mind and body, the intellectual and the sensual, man and the cosmos.

If Nietzsche and Heidegger turn back to the Presocratics, it is because they are still moving in another mental context, in a larger space. The questions the Presocratics are asking are to do with the nature of, and difference between, Being and Becoming, order and disorder. They wonder if change is intrinsic in matter or if it is imposed from some external source. They wander over the world with open eyes and open mind, as in White's poem about one of them, 'Xenophanes of Kolophon':

> Poet and philosopher –
> when the Persians invaded Asia Minor
> he moved to Sicily
>
> walking along the shore of that island
> he wrote:
>
> even if you stumble
> on some rocks of the truth
> you'll never know it all
>
> he spoke of sea, wind, earth
> clouds and rivers
> and said that god was round.[49]

They are atomists, talking about the collision of atoms in an anarchic, godless, lawless universe. For Heraclitus, all is change, 'everything flows'. Fire is the measure of change. White compares Socrates and Heraclitus, saying: 'While Socrates thinks *about* the wave, Heraclitus thinks *as* the wave'[50]. In this, the Presocratics are still Eastern in outlook. White also refers to a Japanese No play where a character walks in contemplation along the shore until he *becomes* the shore.[51] And like Chuang-Tzu the Taoist, the Presocratics are scientists, poets, mathematicians, philosophers, musicians, biologists . . . all at once. They feel part of the wild anarchic swirl of the universe.

The intervening centuries have witnessed a slow and steady decline, accelerating in the Modern Age which has devoted itself to objectivist realism. It is out of this context that real post-modern thought has tried to break.

For Husserl, the founder of Transcendental Phenomenology, objectivism is 'naivety'. In most day-to-day experience we do not perceive reality, we merely *opine*. For Husserl, we must learn to look at things stripped of all that is superfluous, of all that might be called 'opinion', of all that is not phenomenal. This is a process akin to the Buddhist idea of 'emptying the mind'. Let's note, in passing, the first line of one of Kenneth White's shorter poems: *A gull's cry emptied my skull*[52], which is typically humorous in its paradox – presumably the gull's cry filled his skull to the point that, as the closeness of 'gull' and 'skull' underlines, it *became* the gull's cry.

There are obvious pitfalls in Husserl's approach, but there is a stronger energy in the radical shift it achieves. Here, the subject/object dualism disappears, but so does the idealist/materialist dualism. This is not to say that matter does not exist except in our perception, nor to say that it did not exist before *homo sapiens*, nor that it will cease to exist after us, but it is to say that our relationship with the world is extraordinarily intimate, creative and unique. The idealist/materialist dualism is a failure to consummate that relationship and achieve that enlightened position where to look at the world *en gros* or in miniature detail is to look at oneself. These lines from White's 'The Region of Identity' are a striking example of this radical relationship between human perception and the world:

This pool of water
holding rock and sky
traversed by the wing-flash of birds
is more my original face
than even the face of Buddha.[53]

That is a perception wherein day-to-day consciousness is transcended by 'poetic intelligence' (*sophia*). The eye, unencumbered by the distractions of the personal and the social, undeflected by opinion, interpretation and value, can *see this pool of water as it is*, and in doing so, sees a timeless image of the world 'looked at' by the eye which is the pool perceiving *rock and sky* and passing birds, in which it recognises its true, *original* self. And since the reader of these lines cannot but see the same thing as the poetic voice has seen (presuming a similar unencumbered approach to the poem on the part of the reader, which entails a certain amount of *work*), it becomes my, your, our *original face* also, in our contemplation of the poem which communicates the contemplation of the pool of water.

Phenomenology says that the object is apprehended by the subject whose unencumbered attitude will allow it intuitively to grasp the object's essence. This is the attitude that the 'intellectual nomads', whom Kenneth White explores in the essays and creates in his longer poems, come to be aware of. In 'Hölderlin in Bordeaux'[54], for example, the German poet (revisited by White) is restless, unfulfilled in his personal-social context, literary Germany. He wants to go back to another Germany, reduced in the first instance to essentials:

some window overlooking a forest maybe
a little philosophical light

Images of earth and travelling impress upon him and make him wonder about his own poetic journey, but he knows the old methods are done, he can no longer *indulge in that archaic hyperbole/dream the ideal*. And his metaphorical awareness that *the landscape had changed*, loses its metaphorical distancing as he pictures again where it was that he had realised this:

he'd felt it crossing Auvergne
that awful night
losing his way
in the ice and snow
he'd felt it
the landscape had changed
colder
craggier
more massive –
poetry itself would have to change

His early idealism broken, Hölderlin realises that there are 'no gods to sing to', but 'a nothingness to face', and the new void, as is made plain by the ephemeral images of the city of Bordeaux:

seeing at some high window
a beautiful face
that was there, then gone

is something to be travelled *alone*. The rhythm of the poem, mirroring its content, becomes slower and more open, becoming calmer as it becomes more aware of the expansive void to which the content has directed itself. It is a rhythmical movement common to many of White's longer poems which present us with types of the 'intellectual nomad', and, ironically, the feeling it evokes carries echoes of the old tragic sensibility – the feelings of pity and terror combined – but only in echo, for the over-riding sense of 'possibilism' in White's work breathes a current of creative energy into all these moments when the void opens up.

And it often centres on the concept of expression: 'poetry itself would have to change'. The big problem posed by transcendental phenomenology is that of inter-subjectivity. Any genuine perception (subjective) becomes itself an object when offered to others (as a poem, say). There is an enormous responsibility for authenticity and integrity, then, on the part of the perceiver, but there is an equally enormous responsibility resting, too, on the reader, the listener, the sharer of that perception.

What excites me about White's work is that, consistently, it breaks down the barriers between poet, poem and reader, offering perceptions with the minimum of essential detail, requiring of the reader a creative intention in approaching the poem which opens up the spaces of the mind in a way which so much of conventional poetry fails to do. Any number of his poems could illustrate this, but here is 'A High Blue Day on Scalpay'[55]:

> *This is the summit of contemplation, and*
> *no art can touch it*
> *blue, so blue, the far-out archipelago*

> *and the sea shimmering, shimmering*
> *no art can touch it, the mind can only*
> *try to become attuned to it*
> *to become quiet, and space itself out, to*
> *become open and still, unworlded*
> *knowing itself in the diamond country, in*
> *the ultimate unlettered light*

When he says:

> *the mind can only*
> *try to become attuned to it*
> *to become quiet, and space itself out*

the echo of 'atoned' ('at-one-ed') in the word 'attuned' makes the reader see the mind *becoming* the

> *blue, so blue, the far-out archipelago*
> *and the sea shimmering, shimmering.*

This is Kenneth White's experience originally, but in its poetic manifestation, stripped of all but its essential phenomenality, the mind depicted becomes the reader's mind, then *the* mind. The poem is encountered by readers whose 'attitude' (in the philosophical sense) allows them to grasp it subjectively, to 'intuit' its essence.

But it is not enough to say that what I read in this poem is a perception of the mind. I *see* the islands and the sea, just as White saw them – the image is concrete and literal at the same time as it is abstract and metaphorical, and it does not make sense unless you see these unities. The experience of the poem is only comprehensible if seen in phenomenological terms in which the mind and the sea off Scalpay are united.

Husserl's pupil, Martin Heidegger, continues his radical overhaul of Western philosophy. If philosophy is the identifying characteristic of the West, its fundamental question is, 'Why are there things which exist rather than nothing?' In surveying 2,500 years of thinking he discovers that the key notion here, *being*, has been too much of a thorny idea for our great thinkers. Hegel makes it the 'universal concept', Kant calls it the 'categorical imperative', both of which conveniently put it out of the way. For Nietzsche, *being* was a 'smoky vapour'. For Heidegger, it can neither be absent nor dissipated because all things which exist depend upon it, so he tries to *re-ground* it. He traces the history of the idea of *being* as it unravelled in Western thought into four distinctions:

    i) *being and becoming*
    ii) *being and appearance*
    iii) *being and thinking*
    iv) *being and ethics.*

If we are to understand *being*, we must understand why these distinctions arose but, more importantly, we must accept that the fact that they arose means they were originally united, and try, then, to restore them to their original ground.

As Heidegger does this, he reconstructs the basic concepts in Western thought and shows that in their original form they were quite different from the way we understand them. Their original form is Presocratic, that initial burst of philosophical energy which was turned onto a metaphysical plane by Plato. The table

below gives the original Presocratic meanings on the left and
their platonic and modern development on the right:

Presocratic		Postsocratic
truth	= 'standing in the light' or, 'unconcealment'	'opinion', 'moral value'
logos	= 'gathering', or 'collectedness'	'ratio', 'discourse'
noein	= 'apprehend'	'think'
physis	= 'emergence into the light'	'idea'

In Presocratic perception, then, phenomena *emerge, stand,*
and *endure in the light* and are *apprehended* by men. What is
interesting about that is that these original meanings connote
movement, event, experience and presence. What they have
become in Socratic time is static, formulaic, to do with opinion
and interpretation, divided into categories. In Plato a very odd
thing happens when the world of phenomena becomes the world
of *non*-being in opposition to the ideal world of the Forms. What
happened, according to Heidegger, is that while the *foundation*
(Presocratic) of Western philosophy is in the realisation that *the
question of being necessarily embraces the foundation of 'being-
there'* (that is, the grounding of human perception and being),
the *history* (Postsocratic) of Western philosophy derives from a
misinterpretation of this into *man is a rational animal.*

That is, in the Presocratic foundations, man is in intimate,
creative/destructive relationship with being. He is the one who,
to paraphrase Heidegger's reading of the final chorus from
Sophocles' *Antigone*, works on the earth and so opens up those

things which appear to manifestness – sea, earth, birds and animals; he wrests being from concealment (non-being) and he discloses being through language, and that language (not the language of everyday which is opinion) is poetry. *Poetry brings being into the light*. This active, creative/destructive attitude (akin to White's *erotic logic*) is replaced in Platonic metaphysics by the exaltation of thinking and paradigms somehow separate from the phenomenal world. So, an 'original perspective' must be opened up ('original' in both senses) if we are to regain contact with being. As Heidegger puts it, man is *the site which being requires in order to disclose itself* – the *there*, and the language which he will use to disclose being, if his work is authentic, is poetry, an *authentic* poetry. To get at that kind of poetry, the mind has to travel many roads, and the work never loses sight of the way.

This brings us to some of White's ways, West and East.

6. On American Trails

In Kenneth White's mind, there has for long been a clear distinction between America and U. S. civilisation. The latter interests him hardly at all. America interests him a great deal. He is an 'americanist' in the original sense of that word – a student of the geography and ethnology of America. A whole section of his library, as I've seen it in his Breton house (what he calls his 'Atlantic library'), is devoted to this material, with, among many others, books such as James Frazer's *The Native Races of America* and Franz Boas' *Kwakiutl Ethnography*. He is well versed in all kinds of Americana, taking in, for example, the great explorations of Humboldt, the art of Karl Bodmer, and the canoe routes of the French-Canadian *voyageurs*, often accompanied by Scots. Many a text of White's, poem or prose, has emerged from these studies. Others have had their origin in a series of trips to North America, not by any means across the whole continent, but to particular areas of attraction, notably the north of Northern Canada, and the islands of the Caribbean.

With regard specifically to literature, White has said that, right from the start, and as a Scot, he was more attracted to American literature than to English literature – because it had more space and energy.

As an adolescent, he was a great reader of Emerson's essays, especially from Volume III of a *Collected Works* of Emerson[56], picked up by his father from a book-barrow in Glasgow: essays such as 'Society and Solitude', 'The American Scholar', 'The Method of Nature'. Later, as a student, he was both surprised and delighted to discover that Nietzsche, in whose work he was then immersed, had also been a great reader of Emerson. White may seem on occasion to be moving in all directions, but there's an underlying thread all the time.

After Emerson's essays came Whitman's *Leaves of Grass*, bought by the young White from the shelves of a second-hand bookshop, and the revelation for him that poetry could have a lot more scope, and larger intentions, than anything he had seen up to that time. Whitman was one of the first in the Modern Age to attempt to reunite poetry with science (and with philosophy, in Whitman's case largely Hegelian): 'Exact science and its practical movements are no checks on the greatest poet, but always this encouragement and support.'[57] Close to Whitman in White's mind was Melville, whose enormous research into all manner of sciences and philosophies for the writing of *Moby Dick – the White Whale* is well documented. And next to them was Thoreau, who kept one ledger for his poems, one for his scientific notes (on meteorology, tree growth, etc.), feeling all the time he was out for a unity transcending those separate unities – a unity which, as White shows in his essay on Thoreau in his 'introduction to geopoetics', *Le Plateau de l'albatros*, takes place beautifully, in his most accomplished, most 'complete' texts.

All this is latent, and at times explicit, in White's *The Blue Road*, which is 'the good red road' of the Indians but seen in a darker light. As with all of White's 'waybooks', as he calls them, there is an itinerary at the base, but there is always in them more than an itinerary, with its incidents and encounters, there is a whole world on the move – which takes the waybook way out beyond most travel writing. Here, the itinerary goes from Montreal, along the north bank of the St. Lawrence, up into Labrador, culminating in a wild snowstorm on Ungava Bay. I spoke of a whole world on the move. In this book, it is not only the whole of America that is on the move, from the first crossing of the Bering Strait to the scenes at Montreal and Goose Bay, it is the whole evolution of the Western mind since Romanticism. Again, there are discrete indications as to this possible reading of the book – in the title itself (the 'blue road' is in parallel to the 'blue flower' of Novalis) and in passing quotations from Keats and others, right up via Wittgenstein to that area which White has at various times called 'white world' ('white', that is uncoded) or atopia (as distinguished from that historical projection which is 'utopia').

So, White has studied America, at all levels. He has also taught Americana.

Active in several universities in France, after teaching French literature in Scotland, he was teaching mainly American literature.

Before looking more closely at what he taught, a word concerning the writer as teacher. It is customary among writers to despise, or at least feign to despise, teaching, and 'academic' is currently a pejorative term. White's attitude and activity is entirely different. He has always considered teaching, not as some onerous adjunct, but as the oral extension of his writing. One can go further, and say that teaching for White is part of his cultural activism. As to 'academic', if White can exercise all the qualities of the best academic discipline: solid documentation, clarity of thought, cogent presentation, he is very far from 'the academic' in any desiccated sense of that word. He is closer to Charles Olson, who says: 'The poet is the only pedagogue left to be trusted. And I mean the tough ones, only the very best.'[58]

The second volume of Kenneth White's monumental French State thesis devoted to 'intellectual nomadism' concentrated on America as 'nomad land' and to certain writers White considered as at least to some degree 'intellectual nomads', under the title *Poetry and the Tribe*.[59]

When White came to occupy the Chair of Twentieth-Century Poetics at the Sorbonne, with an entirely free hand to decide what was to be taught and how, he set up a research seminar and a general lecture course.

With very few exceptions (Yeats, MacDiarmid, D. H. Lawrence), these lectures under the title 'fields of energy', were devoted to a selected group of American poets comprising Walt Whitman, T. S. Eliot, Wallace Stevens, Robinson Jeffers, Hart Crane, Allen Ginsberg, Charles Olson and Gary Snyder. All of these were American, but were working against the stream of U.S. civilisation and with radical criticism of 'the American dream'. As general epigraph to these lectures, White often referred to T. S. Eliot's Cape Ann poem:

> *Resign this land at the end, resign it*
> *To its true owner, the tough one, the sea-gull*
> *The palaver is finished.*[60]

While presenting the work of all these poets completely and honestly, White was leading, via them, into the field of his own poetics, which he developed and exposed further, in a more highly individual way, in his research seminar. It was all part of a large, ongoing process.

7. Investigations into Asia

That Asia has played a great role in the opening of White's space is obvious – it's obvious in the poems, in the waybooks (at least two of which move on Asian ground), and is explicit in some of the essays. At one point, he referred to his mental continent as 'Euramerasia', with Asia both as background and as ultimate area. But it is important to go into this in some detail and with a maximum of precision, in order to rid the context of conventional images and conceptions, and to see exactly why Asia attracted White, what he got from it, and how he is situated within the flux of influence that Eastern culture has had on the West, since, say, the eighteenth century, when the first translations from the Sanskrit began to appear, soon to be followed by others from China and, later, Japan.

What has to be said first, in general terms, is that, while White has read massively in Eastern literature, including some of the more difficult texts rarely referred to, he was never out to be an orientalist scholar. 'To be that', he says in *Pilgrim of the Void*[61], 'has never been my aim', defining himself rather as 'a late-modern Western writer, that is, a mind-traveller, looking for new ways of thinking, writing and being'. If the prime motivation was not scholarly, it was also not religious, as it has been with many Westerners. White has never considered 'converting' himself to some system of belief or practice, he has never looked for a guru, indeed, while showing sympathy for people living on those lines, he has also made fun of many aspects of the attitudes arising from these motives. Thirdly, while absorbing a great deal and using material and methods both in poetics and in thought, he has also avoided the more obvious literary influences. There is very little overt reference to the gods and goddesses of Hindu mythology, or to Buddha. And, while practising the haiku, and recommending it, he is not one to frequent the haiku circles that have arisen all over Europe and America, or contribute regularly to the many haiku magazines filled up largely with what he calls 'sheep's trintles'[62].

The Eastern texts he favours (the 'whispered teachings' of Tibetan Buddhism, the 'white line' of Milarepa and Marpa, the most iconoclastic Zen texts, the wild extravagances of Tchuang-tzu . . .) are those which set aside all belief-systems and all ritual practices. Long years of study of certain Eastern texts led him also to a new investigation of the West. He describes for example David Hume, his Scottish compatriot, as:

> . . . so close at times to Buddhist thought, and in particular to its conception of the void, that it makes his Treatise on Human Nature sound like a Scottish version of Nagarjuna.[63]

It is possible to go even further, and to say that White has tried to go back beyond the division of East and West. His ethno-historical investigations (via, among many others, J. G. Frazer) led him back into that 'vagina of the nations', the Eurasian steppe. It is there he discovered shamanism. If he was able to trace shamanic elements in Western literature, specifically Scottish literature, he also saw the distant origin of the Buddhist 'bird path' (the move out of personal identity) in the ornithological itinerary (marked by posts bearing bird wings) of the shaman. Not that this prolonged interest in shamanism meant with White any 'conversion' to shamanism, or any overt imitation of shamanist practices. As already indicated, what he worked out in this context was what he referred to as 'an abstract shamanism'.

With that preliminary mapping of White's 'Eastern field' or 'Asian area' done, we can look at how his 'way' is situated within certain broad reaches of the East–West relationship over the past few centuries.

Let's look at it first at the most abstract level. The philosophy of Heidegger is operating in a field which occasions enormous difficulties for us in the West. We do not have an adequate language for it. It is confusing for us to try to separate this Being from those things which are in a state of being; the capital letter invites the sort of idealism which Heidegger is, presumably, trying to avoid. It is a more adequate language which many minds in the West have sought for in the East. For there we find that, while similar problems are being wrestled with, tradition has never lost sight of the grounding, the unity-in-diversity, an intimacy of perception. It seems to me that when Heidegger speaks of Being he is talking about something similar to the Tao, for example. Husserl's transcendental phenomenology and Heidegger's re-grounding of Being have the effect of re-*orient*ing the West.

But the thing is, maybe, as White would say, to get on the road, to get out on the way. This is precisely what the White poem 'A Fragment of Yellow Silk'[64] invites us to do:

> *Among all that display*
> *of ancient treasure*
> *one thing remains in my mind*
>
> *a fragment of yellow silk*
>
> *hardly bigger*
> *than a breast or a hand*
>
> *unearthed on the road*
> *from Ch'ang to Antioch*
> *via Samarkand.*

On the way we shall meet sudden shifts in thought, and radical developments in artistic, poetic practice.

The discovery of one print by Hokusai (about whom White published a fascinating book in 1990), *The Great Wave at Kanagawa*, inspired Debussy's *La Mer* and influenced Western art forms. Imagism was sourced in Eastern poetry and was the vital shift in modern poetry from the mere practice of language to the cultivation of perception. Tao, Buddhism, Zen . . . whatever the name, the characteristic seems to be an unwavering sense of the here-and-now as the locus of reality and a conscious and rigorous cultivation of perception as the way to discover it. In the Hsieh-i ('writing-meaning') school of painting which was a Taoist reaction to the Kung-pi ('laborious brush') academic tradition, calligraphic brushes and gestures were used to paint landscapes. The calligraphic spirit thus informing the paintings gave the spectator a subtle sense of significance in the landscape so painted. The effect of this style is similar to that which operates in haiku poetry and in the poetry written by White.

One of Kenneth White's most important Eastern references, Basho, started from a tradition which had, as in the West, elevated the metaphor and a pleasing use of words. He developed this into a new type of poetry combining *substance* and *essence*. This development mirrors the movement in meditation which tends to begin by producing metaphor, but eventually reaches *muga* when the disciple is not looking *at* the object any longer, but is looking as it. Here is Kenneth White as meditant:

> *It was the cold talk of the gulls he liked*
> *and rain whispering at the Western window*

long days, long nights
moving in
to what was nameless
(though the walls were hung with maps
and below him
lay a library of science)

Outside
at the end of that dark winter
he saw blue smoke, green waters
as he'd never seen them before
they were enough
a black crow busy on a branch
made him laugh aloud
the shape of the slightest leaf
entertained his mind
his intellect
danced among satisfactory words. [65]

Here, again, as often with White, we can observe an aural perception: 'cold talk of gulls', 'rain whispering', moving towards a visual perception of the world which results from that sound meditation: 'he saw blue smoke, green waters/as he'd never seen them before'. This perceiver is at one with the world he perceives – he laughs with the crow, he finds joy in the 'thisness' of the leaf and sees the leaf's joy in its own 'thisness' (Duns Scotus' *haecceitas*). All this and his mind and its words dance together.

White often quotes Basho's advice about the pine-tree: 'learn of the pine/from the pine'[66]. Here is the whole of that passage in which the Japanese poet has so much to say about perception, knowledge and expression:

Go to the pine if you want to learn about the pine or to the bamboo if you want to learn about the bamboo. And, in doing so, you must leave your subjective preoccupations with yourself. Otherwise you impose yourself on the object and do not learn. Your poetry issues of its own accord when you and the object have become one – when you have plunged deep enough into the object to see something like a hidden glimmering there. However well-phrased your poetry may be, if your feeling is not natural – if the object and yourself are separate – then your poetry is not true poetry but merely your subjective counterfeit.[67]

In a workshop for psychiatrists and psychoanalysts held in Mexico in the late 1950s, the Japanese Zen authority, Daisetz Suzuki, compared two poems, one by a Westerner, Alfred Lord Tennyson, and the other by the Japanese poet Basho (1644–1694).[68]

Here is Basho's poem:

> *When I look carefully*
> *I see the nazuna blooming*
> *by the hedge!*

Tennyson's is this:

> *Flower in the crannied wall,*
> *I pluck you out of the crannies;*
> *Hold you here, root and all, in my hand,*
> *Little flower – but if I could understand*
> *What you are, root and all, and all in all,*
> *I should know what God and man is.*

The subject matter is, on the surface, the same, but the Westerner who requires to question and get all wordy about the flower, kills it in order to do so. The 'thinking' (metaphysical, religious, anthropocentric) man destroys the phenomena of the world. Basho, on the other hand, merely looks at the flower 'carefully', *sees* it and allows his feeling to remain silent inviting you, the reader, to reach the same feeling by achieving the same perception. Like the experience it conveys, the poem requires to be entered into by contemplation just as Basho enters into the flower, because, since he looks 'carefully' at it, he sees it not as a static decoration on the hedge, but as a living thing – he sees its 'blooming', *feels* that 'blooming' because *he has become the flower and has made the flower expressive of its being.* When you enter into that experience also, by contemplating the poem, you become the 'I' of the poem, everyone becomes the 'I' of the poem, this *one* particular perceptual experience contains *all* perceptual experience in it. As Suzuki puts it:

> I, you, he, she or it – all this is a pronoun standing for the somewhat behind it. Who is this somewhat?

The haiku works as a sign, a gesture, a nudge which pushes you out of yourself and into the whole, while Tennyson extirpates the flower in order to express his 'personality' at all costs. The poem that has the more to say, that opens up a cosmology, is the poem which says nearly nothing, which just does not look like 'a poem' at all.

Here is what Suzuki has to say of Tennyson:

> There is in the first place, no depth of feeling; he is all

115

intellect, typical of Western mentality. He is an advocate of
the Logos doctrine. He must say something, he must
abstract or intellectualise on his concrete experience. He
must come out of the domain of feeling into that of intellect
and must subject living and feeling to a series of analyses to
give satisfaction to the Western spirit of inquisitiveness.

Although White would perhaps take issue with Suzuki's
rather glib use of Western philosophical vocabulary, he would
agree wholeheartedly with the general tenor of this statement. It
is a pretty devastating picture: thought with no feeling, man alien
in his world, pathetic questioning as an end in itself. It is,
perhaps, one could add, a little unfair in its starkness – if you
wanted to choose a poet to demonstrate the capacity for banality
and word-death in the West you'd find few better candidates
than the man Joyce called Alfred Lawn Tennis Shoes. But the
general point is apt if the illustration is a little easy and the
thought and expression of Tennyson here is Western
commonplace.

It was to get out of this Western commonplace that Yeats
worked on and with the Upanishads[69], in the process getting rid
of his early mythologising and metaphorising and learning to
'walk naked'[70]. It was in a similar way, with a parallel intention,
that Ezra Pound worked on the translations and notes of Ernest
Fenollosa concerning Chinese and Japanese language and
poetry[71], he also getting rid of his early aestheticising, learning to
see 'bare trees on the skyline' and, from out of this
phenomenology, 'make cosmos'[72].

It is this question of 'cosmos' (world) that is ultimately
paramount in White's thought and poetics. Pound did not make
it, getting lost in what White calls 'a farrago of history'. However

beautiful are Yeats' images of Ireland, it is hard to say he arrived at anything like 'world', remaining attached to glebe and blood. However detached he was from those identifications, however much he worked on universalist principles (largely linguistic), it is hard to say that Joyce made it.

One of the things that distinguish White from these predecessors, whom he salutes, is his interest in science. This interest in science, outside any positivistic scientism, not only helps to keep him free of all kinds of imaginative (and religious, and political) aberrations, but provides him with possibilities of language outside metaphor and indeed many of the other components of conventional (and less conventional) verse.

To come back to Fenollosa, whom White studied thoroughly, here he is on the noun-verb relationship:

> A true noun, an isolated thing, does not exist in nature. Things are only the terminal points, or rather, the meeting points of actions, cross-sections cut through actions, snapshots. Neither can a pure verb, an abstract notion, be possible in nature. *The eye sees noun and verb as one:* things in motion, motion in things.

This is a theory of perception. But we are close here to the reality of quantum physics: the impossibility of saying whether primal energy is particle or wave.

8. Pathways in Science

Kenneth White has frequently said (and the signs are there) that he has always read as much science as he has literature. When he still used, at least in passing, the term 'metaphysics', he would say that there was a lot of physics in his metaphysics. Facts from geology, biology, botany, ornithology abound in his texts. And the type of thinking he practises has affinities with scientific thinking. 'Logic' is a word frequent with him – he will talk, for example, of 'the logic of Lannion Bay'[73], to refer to all the various forces at play in a stretch of water and to the difficult-to-grasp configurations that result. He will at times call this logic 'erotic logic', or speak of 'erotocosmology'. This linguistic extravagance is no mere neologistic word-play, it indicates the poet's feeling his way out into new dimensions.

Concerning the new dimensions opening up in science since, say, Quantum Theory, Karl Popper, in *The Logic of Scientific Discovery*[74], has this:

> Every physical measurement involves an exchange of energy between the object measured and the measuring apparatus . . . A ray of light, for example, might be directed upon the object and part of the dispersed light reflected by the object might be absorbed by the measuring apparatus. Any such exchange of energy will alter the state of the object which, after being measured, will be in a state different from before. Thus the measurement yields, as it were, knowledge of a state which has just been destroyed by the measuring process itself [. . .] therefore the measurement cannot serve as a basis for prediction.

In general terms directly applicable to the sort of poetry which Kenneth White has been aiming for, this means *there can be no objective view of reality because you cannot separate the perceiver from the perceived.*

Quantum Theory arose out of a meeting of two initially separate strands of research: Heisenberg's on the particle electron, and Schrödinger's development of de Broglie's wave theory, both read extensively by White.[75] Statistical interpretation of these theories found them to be interchangeable – wave as particle, particle as wave. This leads to some quite alarming (for scientists) conclusions. For Heisenberg it meant that an 'objective' physics, i.e. a sharp division of the world into object and subject, had ceased to be possible. As for Niels Bohr, he took the implications further, saying that what was involved was not merely a change in mechanical and electrical-dynamic theories, but the failure of even our most sophisticated spatio-temporal images to describe natural phenomena.

With measurement and prediction becoming impossible and with object-subject and space-time dualisms collapsing, science, as we understand it, would seem to collapse also, or, rather, move into another field. Karl Popper published his *Logic of Scientific Discovery* in order to save science from either of these possibilities. His book is an attempt to restate the grounding of science, to found a theory of the 'demarcation' of physics through the key concept of 'falsifiability'. This is to keep physics apart from metaphysics. He deplores 'inductive thinking', that is, the movement from immediate sense-perception to 'universal statements', as being 'metaphysical' or 'psychologism'. He restates the conventional scientific preference for 'deductive thinking', i.e. the formulation of hypotheses which are tested in the sense-field. An empirical view of the world can only be achieved, according to Popper, from this deductive method. I can only say *this is a glass of water* (describing thus an immediate sense-perception) if I already understand the words *glass* and *water* in a *universal* sense first. For Karl Popper, perception is the testing of theory – as he puts it, you don't expect an audible noun along with a tactile verb.

Now, we would want to go along with this scientist's argument some of the way, since we never want to lose track of intellectual rigour. But what Karl Popper was really trying to do was to put bounds on a field of knowledge just at the moment when it was attempting an authentic and great leap. Can we follow quantum physics into the new, anarchic, open world it has discovered, where dualisms and the specialist boundaries of rationalism collapse, while at the same time, retaining a sense of perspective, of context, without losing sight of reality and reducing our means of perception only to 'signs' and 'texts'? Does the 'object' have to disappear totally with 'objecti*vism*'?

Let's turn to Kenneth White's significantly entitled poem 'Theory'[76], to which he adds this footnote, which confronts Popper's stance, suggesting, perhaps, that true perception comes out of the play between inductive and deductive thinking, both being necessary:

> The word 'theory' in this poem may seem totally out of place [. . .]. Maybe this poem goes back to a more primordial sense of theory, the one still present in Aristotle when he says that life spent in theory is a kind of divine life, *ontologically extraordinary*.

That last phrase, 'ontologically extraordinary', is a recurrent one in White's writing, as in, for example, the 'extraordinarily ontological territory' of 'Mountain Study'.

Here is the poem of the new scientific-ontological-poetic theory:

> *1.*
> *The white cell almost in darkness*
> *outside: rocks in disruption, sea-*
> *silence wavering. It is there.*
>
> *2.*
> *Rough shape, clifted, that quartz*
> *chaos-given, ashored, tide-washed and*
> *in the good space gazed-at*
>
> *3.*
> *Cast – the first stone; only the*
> *thrust and the not-silver, not-white, not-crystal*
> *splash – no reading in the widening circles.*
>
> *4.*
> *Great reason grasped, the twelve-worded orator*
> *walks on the shingle*
> *with quiet eyes.*

Here, the poetic voice is describing 'sense-perceptions' on the face of it. But it is neither inductively moving from there to a 'universal statement', nor is it coming at the sense-perceptions with a theory to test – rather, both things arise at the same time. What happens is an *event* in which an immediate sense-perception (sound of sea, gazed-at quartz, splashing water) and (to use that inadequate scientific vocabulary) a 'universal statement' (*great reason*), are 'grasped' at the same time. The concrete experience and the abstract thought or awareness are not separate but arise together in the perception of the poet. That is the significance of what might seem to some the loose and a-poetic, but, in fact, poetically energised phrase, *It is there* – there is a lot of Being in that little word 'It', a lot of the experiential universe in that small word 'there'. And it is all quietly underlined by the parallel shaping of the first three sections in images of *rock, sea, sight*, moving in the last section into *reason, shore, clarity*, each line coming in like a wave.

We still live in a world dictated by Newtonian physics, the only 'normal' relief from which lies in imagination or fantasy (themselves often determined by the world-system they try to escape from). With Newton, Nature has become machine. The typical dynamic image is the clock ('clocks all over the cancerous landscape', says White in *Travels in the Drifting Dawn*[77]) – it is a condition of equilibrium, reducible to small parts, the analysis of which is enough to provide the picture of the whole. This image fitted beautifully into the Reformed, Rationalist, about-to-be-industrialised age because it gave the new world a religious compatibility. If the world is a clock, then God is a watchmaker, necessary but invisible, detached and perceivable in one's awareness of the universal law which governs things. It is all wonderfully convenient.

The picture is awesome. In Pascal it engenders panic and in John Donne a sensation of lost relationship.[78] Newton accelerates the alienation from Nature, since, with him, the human being is an independent observer of the universe from outside. What the scientist wants to achieve is the position of what Laplace called the 'demon' – one who could be in such a position that all the universal laws would be perceived, or, ideally, *the* universal law would become apparent. In other words, the scientist invites man into God's distant, objective viewpoint. We come to an equation in which Nature is simply no longer there. This is not Man *in*, or even Man *and* Nature, this is Man and God (the Christian God of course) and all is symmetry and clockwork order.

There was some criticism of it. In France, a vitalist school grew up and its leading figure, Diderot (a figure dear to White), demonstrated the ridiculous nature of Newton's claims to a world vision by emphasising the importance of growth and development in biological forms, and the idea of man in nature. He advised the pursuit of chemistry and the abandonment of physics, but this view was to be buried for a hundred years or more. What occurred was a split between science and philosophy – the encyclopedic perspective[79] was abandoned in favour of specialism. Within science itself, what we witness is the split between the 'true' classical physics of dynamics and the other sciences of chemistry and biology which pursue, separately, their own, 'inferior' paths (paths which White would follow, developing from them what he called at one point 'biocosmopoetics'[80]).

Later in the eighteenth century, Kant gave these splits theoretical order with his phenomena-noumena division, whereby science dealt with the phenomena of matter while the mind, whose perception apprehends that matter, transcends such mundane tasks in the great spirit of philosophy. For Kant, the subject is at the centre of things. If science has occupied the objective centre-ground, philosophy moves into the subjective height. The result, a split mind.

The beginnings of a move away from classical dynamics comes in 1811 with Fourier's theory of heat, which led to the development of thermodynamics. In this system, heat is the measure of change and as scientists have to face up to the uncomfortable fact that heat or energy has a universal tendency to be lost, the theory of entropy is proposed to cater for this. Entropy theory proposes that all systems move towards degradation, disorder and death. This means that we have to take account of what Eddington calls the 'arrow of time'. As the theories of thermodynamics develop, the studies of chemistry and biology, etc. begin to move centre stage again as notions of equilibrium in Newtonian physics are invited to countenance the possibility of non-equilibrium states and the consequent fact that matter is not passive but active. If this is an advance in knowledge, it is also a return to previous knowledge: the dialectics of order and disorder, being and becoming, the sense of movement and change in Heraclitus.

The nineteenth century was taken up, then, with a theoretical struggle between dynamics and thermodynamics, scientists being anxious to explain away the apparent problems for the Newtonian world-view posed by entropy. The scientific quarrel was reflected in the human world. The perfect order with everything in its place was having some difficulty sustaining its credibility in the world it had allowed to evolve. The friendly machine of the piston had been replaced by the steam engine and the industrial revolution had turned the heavens of human contemplation into an inferno. A further split in the scientific world came with Darwin's theory of evolution, for it appeared incompatible with the law of entropy. As opposed to entropy's inexorable move towards degradation and death, Darwin showed that all biological systems evolve towards higher and higher levels of complexity.

The idea of an attractor was introduced: the notion that systems are attracted towards a state of equilibrium. And Boltzmann developed the theory of probability to explain what was to be called equilibrium thermodynamics: by bringing a measure of statistical predictability into systems it was hoped to reconcile dynamics and thermodynamics. In the twentieth century these lines of argument proceeded towards Relativity Theory. This arose from the idea of constraint. In Einstein's case, the speed of light is a universal constraint; it plays a part in what we see. Here begins the idea, as opposed to classical physics, that the observer is part of that which he observes. Einstein however, still insisted that relativity made no difference to the idea of universal laws, time was still irrelevant, systems still reversible. In these movements from Thermodynamics to Relativity Theory we can see a return to a position of man *and* nature. Symmetry is still perceived as the order of things, but rather than static deterministic laws we have a recognition of change as process.

This is where the poet, banished from science, comes back in – not as sentimentalist, not as fantasist, not as linguistic juggler, but as conceptor (White's geopoetics is a concept), and as creator of language. We could also add, with reference to White's complete field, de-conditioner (the 'supernihilist').

With this caveat, as White takes care to point out, if there is no 'divine', universal view available, or possible, this does not mean the total, wholesale acceptance of all 'points of view', or all conceptions of the world, any kind of fantasy. First of all, the relativity of Einstein takes place within a world already disengaged from myth, magic and personal projection. Then, one can, in a work, multiply the points of view, which is exactly what White does in his waybooks. And lastly, as White insists, what ultimately counts is the point of view which opens the largest perspective, provides the deepest sense of world.

Our education and upbringing are still largely determined by an outdated world-view. Our perceptions, instilled in us at birth are at odds with the real world and if we are to liberate ourselves from this, we need to decondition ourselves – a process that is not without danger. We are caught between our intrinsic awareness of alienation, of having lives divorced from reality and our fear of the unknown into which we step when we attempt to liberate ourselves.

The modern world, then, is an unnatural development of one-sided experience, specialisms at all levels of society, the cultivation of order, aiming for the Ideal, the order imposed by religion and history, right and left.

White's geopoetics starts from the standpoint that man is inseparably in nature and that knowledge and experience are multi-faceted. In fact, geopoetics would quickly move away from these very words as too redolent of the established ways of thinking, the intellectual constructions of alienation. The very word 'nature', even a phrase such as 'man in nature', contains in its form our separation from the world. The word 'environment' has a similar effect – while seeming to mark a concern for the natural world, it in fact retains a separate humanity at the centre of it. Likewise, 'ecology' is limited in its usefulness because, as a word, it inscribes itself in all the other *-logies* of the specialising, classificatory system.

In White's vocabulary, instead of man-in-nature, environment and ecology, we find 'biocosmopoetics', 'open world poetics', and, finally, 'geopoetics': the concept which underpins our perception of reality, the lines of experience we trace in our lives, the expression that this all leads to. This goes beyond idealism and specialism, beyond humanism and rationalism, beyond all the -isms which are static, to a fluid and concentrated movement of thought, practice and expression. Thought becomes cartography, practice a 'way', and expression a natural event culminating from these movements the way a flower, a mountain, a creature is the concentrated expression of the landscape, the world space in which it emerges into the light out of concealment, to use the Presocratic vocabulary. Here we begin to see in its full light the multiplicity of White's physical and mental explorations, as well as the nature of his writing.

In the Prologue to his book on Scotland, *Écosse, le pays derrière les noms* ('the land behind the names'), Kenneth White evokes an interview in which a journalist, inviting him to talk about his Scottish origins and what they meant to him and his work, starts talking about bards, ghosts, and loch monsters, the usual set of commonplaces, till White cuts him off. He then imagines a more informed and intelligent interlocutor saying something like this: 'Kenneth White, you come from the land of James Clerk Maxwell, the man who opened the way not only to Hertz and Marconi, but also to Einstein and Quantum Physics, who, on the basis of his studies on the interaction between the electric and the magnetic fields, invented the electromagnetic theory of light. Does this idea of "interactive fields" have any reference to your own work?'

Since this book on White is written in Scotland, it seems appropriate to extend our incursion into the science field in the company of James Clerk Maxwell, and another Scottish scientist, to whom White is singularly close, D'Arcy Thompson.

James Clerk Maxwell developed a theory of 'singular points', that is points which systems reach where the laws of deterministic dynamics break down and motion and change become indeterminate. The amount of energy required at these singular points to reach a new configuration or form can be extremely small and yet have massive effects. He talks about how a rock can be loosed by a small movement in frost crystals which can detonate a devastating amount of energy, how a little spark starts a forest fire, a word a war, how one spore blights an entire crop.

Maxwell's work was not considered important because it could not be understood in the context of his time. It is seen now as an important precursor of recent developments and of geopoetics. This new science replaces the closed networks of dynamics with open systems exchanging energy with the environment. Far-from-equilibrium (i.e. unstable, anarchic, chaotic) conditions reach what are called 'bifurcation points' where chance allows 'fluctuations' to push the system towards a new order called 'dissipative structures'. In the most complex, unstable systems appear 'strange attractors' adding to the chaotic unpredictability of the process. We are talking, then, about an amount of self-organisation which implies some form of 'communication' within molecular systems. Life arises out of these disordered, chaotic turbulences. Dissymmetry, disorder and chance are the characteristics of life; equilibrium, symmetry and determinism are the characteristics of death. How this applies to poetics, and in particular to geopoetics, to White's writing in general, seems obvious enough. Order (shape, form) is not imposed on matter, matter itself, the world is auto-poetic, and the thing for the poet is to listen into it, tune into its wavelength.

Then there is the biologist and morphologist, D'Arcy Thompson. In an essay that is part of *On Scottish Ground*[81], White quotes these extracts from Thompson's *On Growth and Form*:

> The waves of the sea, the little ripples on the shore, the sweeping curve of the sandy bay between the headlands, the outline of the hills, the shape of the clouds, all these are so many riddles of form, so many problems of morphology. Apart from the physical-chemical problems of physiology, the road of physico-mathematical or dynamical investigation in morphology has found few to follow it; but the pathway is old. The way of the old Ionian physicians, of Anaxagoras, of Empedocles and his disciples in the days before Aristotle, lay just by that highway side.

It is easy to see just how much scientific pages such as this meant to the young White when he was trying to follow out the lines he knew from the Fairlie shore and hills. When, later in France, White read René Thom[82] (who in fact registers his debt to Thompson), he could not but see a connection between Thompson's work and the work of that mathematician, another boundary crosser, who attempts to relate theoretical mathematics to living biology and in doing so moves into the fields of philosophy and linguistics. Here is a page of René Thom's, describing life at work which is singularly reminiscent of Thompson's page both in tone and structure:

> The solar photons arriving in contact with the soil and seas are immediately stopped, and their energy abruptly degraded into heat, in this way, the discontinuity of the earth and water surface is also a shock wave, a cliff down which the negentropy of the sun's rays falls. Now life can be considered as some kind of underground erosion of this cliff, smoothing out the discontinuity; a plant, for example is nothing but an upheaval of earth towards the light, and the ramified structure of its stem and root is the same as that found when a stream of water erodes a cliff and produces a mound of debris.

This is the kind of reading of the world, and hence writing of the world, that are part integral of geopoetics: the large view combined with detail, the linking of local and global, abstract and concrete, energies emerging into delineated space, force welling up into form.

Here is White the cartographer-cosmographer talking about the topography of Atlantic Scotland, while evoking Humboldt's *Cosmos*, another study, along with Humboldt's *Views of Nature*, very close to White and eminent precursors of geopoetics:

> As Humboldt points out in *Cosmos*, what largely started up and quickened Greek thought was the topography of Hellas: the multiplicity of headlands and islands, the profusion of creeks and bays. Well, that West coast of

Scotland, with its highly irregular outline and its 500 islands, has a similar kind of topography, though, up to now, one can hardly say that it has given rise to a comparably complex thought. [. . .] Lastly, now that we are beginning to hear again of the concept 'Europe', I think it will be as well for it to look to the West, not only as a breathing space, but as the locus (*topos*) of forgotten movements and perhaps a new type of thought, a new sense of culture, a new *logos*.[83]

In an essay on the explorer-cartographer Lapérouse, he talks about the relationship between science and thought in the context of the lively essay-writing of the eighteenth century:

It's an age in which fullness of matter combines with lines of intelligence to create live thought expressed principally in the form of essays, from Hume's *Essay on Human Understanding* to Fabre's *Essai sur la théorie des torrents*. How much more exciting and stimulating than the novels of Tom, Dick and Harry that were to encumber Europe in the two centuries following![84]

In the dispute about order engaged in by these essay writers, Kenneth White echoes the new science when he says:

. . . it probably implies the sense of a moving mind-world, with a sensation of more or less distant harmony and wholeness, but also a readiness to accept breaks, interruptions, fractures.

Turning to literature he notes Lapérouse's comments on Cook's journals, which had been written up by a literary editor:

I've often regretted that [. . .] he borrowed a stranger's

pen. His description of the customs, manners and arts of the various peoples have always seemed to me completely satisfactory, and the account of his navigation have always given me the *revealing detail* I was looking for as a guide to my own. This is the kind of thing that an editor won't respect: for the sake of harmony of phrase, he'll sacrifice the very word a mariner wants and would prefer to the rest of the work. Besides, in this kind of reading, one likes to put oneself in the place of the traveller, whereas all we get with every line is an actor playing his part – no doubt with great elegance and with finer manners, but totally incapable of giving us the real thing. The various chapters were not composed according to the *rhythm of the voyaging*, the sailing plans are presented in a uniform way, whereas when you are engaged in a vast space comprising two hemispheres they are bound to give rise to a *thousand variations*. We miss the instability that comes from the slightest change in circumstance. *The man of letters ends up effacing the traveller completely.* (KW's italics.)

This is where we really get into the reach of White's poetics:

Lapérouse spoke about the end of geography, that is of a time when cartography would no longer be a problem. He was certainly a bit premature there, for even in the simple scientific sense of geography (measuring and situating) there is no doubt still a great deal to be done. Then geography can advance, there can be other geographies. And there can be geopoetics.

The rhythm which you can perceive in that essay, from initial concept to exploration, mental cartography of the vast shoreline of its ideas and implications, and the breakthrough to poetic clarity at the end is one that marks and distinguishes White's work.

In brief, what White has done is to tread paths lying outside the conditioning of our education and upbringing which are still largely determined by the mechanistic world-view and its aftermath. For him, 'post-modern' means a world which has come out of that world-view and its rationalism, dualism, and humanism. Kenneth White's global concept of geopoetics, in reintegrating science and poetics, the fields of knowledge and experience, in working on the language and the rhythms and tonalities required to express this wholeness, achieves a 'sense of world' combining both abstraction and sensation.

9. From Scotland to Alba and Beyond

If, without a doubt, White's main purpose through his life has been the creation of an *opus*, a complete work, seeking the conditions propitious for it, developing it essentially in a kind of isolated *atopia*, it is also true that he has been concerned throughout his life with various particular places, various particular contexts.

Scotland occupies a high position in his list of particular places.

It is in fact the various strands of his relationship to Scotland that constitute the central area, the focal point of White's mental cartography. In the course of his work, he has abstracted this focal area so much that it is applicable anywhere, constituting an energy field with powers of radiation. But its elements are still recognisably Scottish.

When Kenneth White came back to Scotland, it was with that field in mind, and with the idea of 'trying something out' with his native country. In what White thinks of as 'the Alban experiment', he is talking about Scotland, but, back of Scotland, there is Alba, and back of Alba, a territory without a name. If White identifies serious inadequacies in the prevailing cultural context, even in that area supposedly 'radical' (in a purely political sense), he is deeply aware of a larger Scotland, this awareness implying both reconnaissance of the land itself, and the recognition of neglected or forgotten thought-strands.

A useful approach to White's more overtly public field can be made through a questioning of that crucial theme for any society: education. It will be remembered that when White came back to Scotland after his first Paris years, it was, among various other matters and projects ('unfinished business'), to teach at the university. He enjoyed this activity, as did his students, but his judgement of the university as a whole, indeed of the whole educational system, was less than sanguine.

His first feelings on the theme come across in a pamphlet unambiguously entitled 'The Phoney University'[85]. In it he presents the university as a degree factory, intellectually bankrupt and culturally defunct. In the early Welfare State period usually lauded for its expansion of opportunities in education and employment, it is interesting to hear the voice of one of its first generation lamenting the intellectual-cultural poverty which the post-war reforms embodied and propagated:

> Being awake to the real and radical problems is something for which you don't get paid in our society. In fact, you might even lose your job. You might become

unpopular (and that's a terrible thing in Britain where Democracy, which is not democracy, flattens down everything with its million platitudinous feet).

White's engagement with the politics of education was to continue when he returned to France in 1967 and participated, in his own way, in the 'events' of '68. There, other pamphlets he wrote sum up his view of contemporary education systems:

The university is dying underneath its socio-pedagogical structures. The real master-thinkers, life-masters, are never pedagogues. And real students do not subordinate themselves to a pedagogy (the methodological murder of the mind), they follow their desire, right to the end – an over-riding desire for knowledge, understanding and enlightenment.[86]

and give an indication of what he considers a university education system should be:

It may as well be said at the outset, to avoid immediate misconception, that the Creative University will not mean merely, and not even primarily, the encouragement of artistic production, but will foster a general sense of creativity, the development of the possibilities of human being, by a coordinated study of human culture which, instead of leaving the student floundering about, or bogged down, in a cultural mess, will bring him to the point where he can begin seeking creatively on his own [. . .]. The Creative University, then, won't just be another university on the bourgeois pattern, with a Creative Writing school attached. The latter is only a playing to the gallery, or, deeper, a security-system by which excess creativity (according to bourgeois standards) is filtered off into specialist production functions. The Creative University is not based on the idea of mass + artists, but on that of a creative whole, a creative society, and a fully-developed human being [. . .]. The ethos of the Creative University, far from being an ethos of conformity and production, will be an ethos of self-realisation, based on the notion of *auxesis*, the increase of life [. . .]. An author (*auctor*) is, essentially, a man concerned with *auxesis*, and the teachers at the Creative University will be authors in this sense.[87]

In this educational context it is pertinent to explore two peculiarly Scottish thought-systems: Common Sense philosophy and 'democratic intellect', defining White's relationship to them.

In keeping with the spirit of contradiction mentioned above, eighteenth century Scotland, at the moment of her loss of independence, was the centre of an Enlightenment which produced some of the most important work in Europe in the fields of economics (Adam Smith), architecture (James Craig), science (James Watt) and philosophy (David Hume). It was Hume's sharp enquiries and rigorous scepticism which Kant said 'woke me from my dogmatic slumber', and which in his eyes still remain a good starting point. However, Hume's investigations provoked a frightened backlash from the Christian establishment in Scotland in the shape of what was to become known as 'Common Sense Philosophy'. The fundamental assumptions of this doctrine are that 'all knowledge got by reasoning must be built upon first principles', these 'first principles' being common concepts, held 'intuitively' by everyone and not provable but through 'common sense'.

For White, the political and religious strategies behind such a philosophy, particularly in its historical context, are evident. That its major figure was a clergyman, the Rev. Thomas Reid, is no accident. His principle motivation was horror at the implications of Hume's radical scepticism, and his aim was to work out a system that would sound reasonable enough to enlightened, or at least semi-enlightened minds, while maintaining in the background Christian tenets. In other words, White is all for Enlightenment, less for Common Sense Philosophy, and regrets that contemporary Scotland should have stuck to this, instead of rediscovering, following up, and carrying further forward what he considers to be livelier strands, both within the Scottish tradition, and outside it.

On the other hand, that this blockage should have occurred hardly surprises him. Common Sense philosophy obviously ties in more easily with the empiricism endemic to British thought. It is, say its protagonists, a distinctly Scottish contribution to modern thought and 'radicality' as they understand it in politics. What is more, they continue, in order to clinch their arguments in its defence, Scottish Common Sense philosophy played an important role on the European scene, since Victor Cousin, as education minister in the 1830s, made Thomas Reid required reading for French university students.

White is very well aware of this fact, but he sees it in context, and he analyses it – notably in an essay written at the time of the '68 revolt, 'The Origins of the Bourgeois University in France'[88]. Scottish Common Sense philosophy was what the French State of the time thought it needed in order to settle down into post-revolutionary stability, and build up a solid empire, setting aside all the real radicality of the pre-revolutionary thinkers (Rousseau, Voltaire, Diderot). For all of these, it was David

Hume who was the significant Scottish thinker. For White, who also considers Hume to be the active mind, Common Sense philosophy was neither enlightening nor enlivening. Philosophically, it was what White calls 'thick thinking'. It embraces reason (in a smothering kind of way) but eliminates sharpness of thought and exuberance of expression. On the social, political scene, if White is all for 'common sense' (without capitals), the appeal to 'first principles' supposedly intuitively perceived by all will not only never give rise to anything more, at best, than short-term sociological communitarianism, but it can become a bulwark for the most short-sighted political policies imaginable. In addition to that, in White's view, what Common Sense does is benumb with its gravitational ponderousness all the other senses, the play of which, in White's eyes, is the necessary prelude to anything like live thought and live poetics.

In short, for White, Common Sense is a step down from Enlightenment and its possible developments. It is comfortably installed in a context of mechanistic science, with philosophical speculation reduced to humdrum ratiocination, epistemology compartmentalised into discrete categories with little or no need for relation between them and with no grounding to make them coherent. The result is that philosophical speculation and poetic perception which transcend and deepen scientific knowledge are marginalised in, if not expelled from, the world-view. Ironically, Common Sense philosophy finds itself as part of a world vision which denies the generalism and philosophical underpinning which it was supposed to advocate.

Here we move from Common Sense philosophy to an allied but distinct notion, what George Davie calls the Democratic Intellect.[89]

The concept of the Democratic Intellect has become dominant in the main areas of Scottish intellectual life over the last thirty years as a focus for the attempts which have been made to rediscover and re-evaluate our intellectual history and to try to bring some rigour to all areas of cultural life. In the tradition of the Democratic Intellect, all knowledge and experience is grounded in philosophy (both in the etymological sense of the love of knowledge and in the particular sense of a view on the world) and is also aiming towards further philosophical development. It is felt that the needs of the community will be best served by an educational culture whose source and aim is philosophical. The perspective is, then, generalist rather than specialist, and, in education, breadth is espoused and specialisation delayed for as long as possible. The current in fact flows against pure, specialist scientism. In the particulars of a key subject area such as mathematics, the bent is towards geometry rather than algebra. In this mathematical context, William Hamilton's comment seems to illuminate the field:

> The process in the symbolic method (i.e. the algebraic) is like running a railroad through a tunnelled mountain; that in the ostensive (i.e. the geometrical) like crossing the mountain on foot. The former carries us, by a short and easy transit, to our destined point, but in miasma, darkness and torpidity, whereas the latter allows us to reach it only after time and trouble, but feasting us at each turn with glances of the earth and of the heavens, while we inhale health in the pleasant breeze, and gather new strength at every effort we put forth.[90]

Davie's view is that, after two centuries of attack and eroding reforms inspired by anglo-centric views and legislated by Westminster, the boat was sunk. However, any apparent defeat can usher in a latent movement which allows for later re-emergences. If the Scottish mathematicians held on to the pre-eminence of abstractionist geometry, which sees a line as the movement of a point, against atomistic algebra, which sees a line as a series of extensionless points, then perhaps they were proven at least fifty per cent correct to have done so when, a century later, quantum physics came to its revolutionary conclusion that it is impossible to tell whether the basic matter of existence be particle or wave, that is, substance or movement.

Now, a great deal of the foregoing applies to Kenneth White. White's intellectual method is quite clearly generalist and philosophical in nature and his whole life's work could be seen as a development, clarifying and sharpening of the generalist method:

> Davie's book is largely a defence of the Arts Faculty as the living centre of a university, above all specialisms and outside all precocious applications. I go with that – it's a position that's more and more threatened with every passing decade. Then, Davie looks to the Scots-French connection, as representing a mental and existential space which is neither that of bulldog Britain nor that of the Anglo-American world in general. Again I'm with him all the way.[91]

Where White parts company with Davie is with the idea that 'Davie is still out to defend metaphysics' whereas for White, the most interesting and fruitful cultural-intellectual work has been about 'getting out from under metaphysics without falling into flatness'. In other words, while Davie's defence of metaphysics is preferable to the anti-intellectual drift of British culture since the 1940s, if not before, it is what, in another interview, White identifies as a backward step:

> So far, in the history of humanity, culture has been governed by magic, myth, religion or metaphysics – it's only lately it's run down into psychologism, flat sociology, or conceptualism without concept, complacent pathology, linguistic tiddlywinks etc. Take any of the sympathetic movements trying today to improve matters. They're all moving back into the language of magic, myth, religion or metaphysics. Geopoetics tries to move forwards. It's more difficult. It's also a great deal more interesting.[92]

What brought White to the field of geopoetics was what he calls, in distinction to the Democratic Intellect, the Nomadic Intellect. I now wish to examine that concept within the context of Scottish cultural history.

From early on, White's study of locality had brought him into contact with occluded elements of Scottish culture, including those labelled 'Celtic'. This culture had become something of a parody in Britain, mocked and humiliated by the music hall. But enough evidence of its past survived in signs and texts here and there if, like White, you were determined to find them, to suggest that here might be local grounding for the world-view he was seeking. In doing this he was reaching back beyond the greco-roman perception of his locality which is the dominant perspective of Western culture. Later, he was to discover that one who was to reveal himself as a kindred spirit when White went to France, André Breton, had advocated that very thing:

> An atavistic leap brought us to interrogate as to their deep aspirations the human beings of our countries as they might have been before the Greco-Latin yoke weighed down on them.[93]

White points out how discussion of Celtic culture has tended to bring Wales and Ireland to the fore, ignoring Scotland, and that this is an error:

> For Scotland, colonised from the beginning of our era by that particularly adventurous tribe, the Scots, was, in a sense, Ireland's second chance, as America (Whitman, Thoreau, Emerson) took over from England (Wordsworth and Keats). Add to this the fact that the great mixture of races in Scotland, and the very strong survival of Pictish culture, created a cultural situation *sui generis* and particularly interesting. So much so that when it was necessary to perfect the education of a young Irishman, he was sent to Scotland.[94]

In White's copious writings on and references to Scotland (two complete books and a great many articles), it is a Scotland other than the stereotyped country which emerges.

In taking his key step from history to geography, White does not make all those ghosts which haunt the Scottish psyche less potent; on the contrary, by placing them in a wider context, seeing them in a larger space, in a much larger concept of time (earth-time, earth-space), he gives them greater scope.

He begins with the land itself:

> Rock is the primary matter. [. . .] The first inhabitants were lichens and mosses, bog-cotton, birch, holly, pine, hazel, oak . . . And the bear, the deer, the wolf, the red deer, the eagle, the grouse, the snow bunting . . .[95]

In 'Scotia Deserta' he imagines the ice working the land to its present shape:

> *thinking back to the ice*
> *watching it move*
> *from the high middle spine*
> *out into the Atlantic*
>
> *feeling it gouge out lochs*
> *and sculpt craggy pinnacles*
> *and smoothe long beaches*
> *the land emerges*
> *bruised and dazed*
> *in the arctic light*[96]

Here in fact we go back beyond Scotland, into the basics of geomorphology. The land in question is still one of the 'nameless places' with which the protagonist of a similar poem, but set in North America 'in the time of the sagas', 'Labrador'[97], 'has been in love'.

Into this landscape come inhabitants who eventually develop a culture whose oral tradition centres round the figure of Finn. It is a culture closely connected with the natural context, and it is marked by images of whiteness: the name Finn itself means 'the white one'. To this land the first name given is 'Alba' (again 'the white land'). It is from this ground of earth, energy and image that White develops his first poetic synthesis: 'White World', which he both deepens and expands in the years following.[98]

It was this culture which Christianity did not so much replace as subsume, allowing vital aspects of it to continue in the guise of a Christianity thus made quite different from the orthodox version. Many early Celtic poems deal with this conflict between the Finn-culture and Christianity, and White loves quoting them – poems about Finn preferring by far 'the sound of the tide on the pebbles of the shore to the noise of the church bell', or about Celtic poet-teachers saying ironically what a pity it is wise and learned people like themselves should be heading for hell, while 'ignoramuses mount to heaven'.

With Paul as its inspiration and Rome its centre, papal Christianity became a religion of the town from whose culture it derived its ideology and practices and its essentially political nature. It was authoritarian in its doctrine and dogma, tightly structured in hierarchical form and rigid in its thinking. It taught through images of suffering in life and glorified, sometimes gross, images of the after-life. Its foundation stone was the doctrine of Original Sin and its aims were social and intellectual control. It laid the cultural ground for the most rigid, hierarchical, authoritarian economy of feudalism and the development of the European sun-kings, the tyrants of divine right. It closed minds into narrow frameworks of obedience and shut out the pathways of enquiry; it took the feet from intellectual exegesis and sat it in the chair of equivocation; it generated hypocrisy and small-mindedness; it turned the natural world into a lifeless pageant of symbols, the more eagerly expressed the more they could be made to symbolise the various manifestations of 'evil' (the serpent, the beast, the dark forest of the 'savage', night . . .); its saints were canonised in blood and gore.

Celtic Christianity, the hybrid that evolved, moving in a terrain of Pictish and Finn-ian confluences, learning also from the Eastern settlements in Syria and Egypt reputed to be direct descendants of the original Christians, was of a quite different nature. 'Everywhere else,' writes Ernest Renan[99], 'Christianity encountered an initial layer of Greek or Roman civilisation. Here (in the Celtic regions) it found a new ground, a temperament analogous to its own and naturally ready to receive it.' For Renan, the key word here is 'naturally'. He speaks of:

> . . . the quite particular vivacity with which the Celts informed their feeling for nature. Their mythology is simply a transparent naturalism, not that anthropo-morphic naturalism of Greece or India where universal forms, erected into living beings and invested with consciousness, tend more and more to detach themselves from physical phenomena and become moral beings, but a sort of realistic naturalism, love of nature for its own sake.

The quality of perception is evident in this, the desire to see and feel things as they are, not as symbols of the elements in some ideal system, nor as symbols of narrowly human qualities and beliefs as in the classical world myths.

Likewise, in Celtic Christianity, there is no massive edification, but an archipelagical formation, and a movement. It is in movement across the landscape, and European texts constantly refer to those wandering monks who, for centuries, flowed in waves across the continent, teaching, philosophising, establishing monastic cells, moving on. Renan, White's neighbour in Brittany, evokes them as 'masters of grammar and literature to the whole of the West' [. . .], studious philologians and bold philosophers.[100]

The key figure for White is Pelagius (the word 'pelagian' turns up again and again in White's texts, often with several levels of meaning), his key propositions being the rejection of Original Sin and the consequent assertion that individual redemption can be achieved by willpower and through the intellect, as opposed to the desired beneficence of Divine Grace. Pelagian thinking, placing work on oneself before faith, is, therefore, utterly out of step with mainstream Augustinian Christianity.

The history of early Christianity, hence, to a large extent, the early history of Europe until the end of the first millenium, is the history of the struggle between the anarcho-intellectual Celts and the authoritarian-dogmatic establishment, between Free Will and Divine Grace, between the natural world and Original Sin. The weapons used against the Celts were the political trickery of double-talk, the reduction of subtle philosophical contemplation to mere equivocation, and sheer abuse. For Jerome, Pelagius was 'that great mountain dog through which the devil barks'[101]. The Synod of Whitby (663 AD), whose purpose was to put an end to Celtic divergences from the norm, concluded: 'The only people stupid enough to put themselves out of step with the entire world are these Scots and their allies, the Picts and Britons, who inhabit some forlorn islands at the far-flung ends of the ocean.'

It is this critical and crucial stage in Scottish culture that White takes as pivot point, tracing it backwards into the archaic landscape, and tracing it forwards into possible developments, outside any romantic celticism, outside any identity ideology. As to the possible developments, White sees Celtic themes, structures, ideas and expression permeating the European tradition and discerns a pelagian line running through the whole of Western culture.

After Pelagius, there was Erigena, called to France by King Charles le Chauve whose main contribution to the ninth century Renaissance in Europe was to offer John the Scot, known as Erigena, the protection from Rome his pelagian ideas necessitated in return for the completion of a task for which the King could find no other European scholar fit: the translation of Greek and Latin texts, in particular that of the Pseudo-Dionysius.

After Erigena, there was John Duns Scotus whose affirmation of the reality of the things of the earth, their individuality (*haecceitas* or *thisness*), and his central tenet that it is possible to reach 'the divine presence' through knowledge of the material world, are clearly in tune with the Celtic strain.

The line can be traced right up into modernity, with André Breton, in his 'Ode to Charles Fourier', evoking Pelagius in the following terms: 'your head erect over all those bended brows'[102].

Pelagius, Erigena and Scotus are major and constant references for White and it is easy to see why. Their insistence upon the reality of this world, the earth, and upon the possibility of attaining the highest reality through intelligent experience clearly chimes in with White's way of thinking, living and writing.

They touch upon the question of expression in a way which is central to White's concerns as poet and writer. The problem identified by Erigena concerning the language that can express reality remains central: what is the relationship between our perception and the language we use to express it? Is it possible to express essential reality in human language? These are core questions for White's work in general and for geopoetics in particular.

NOTES

1. See 'Affinités aquitaines', in *Le Monde ouvert de Kenneth White*.

2. Notice on Buchanan in David Irving, *The Lives of the Scottish Poets*, London, 1810, one of the many books of and on Scottish literature, from the earliest times on, that feature on the shelves of White's library.

3. 'Looking Out: From Neotechnics to Geopoetics', *On Scottish Ground*, p. 129–147.

4. From Geddes' text 'An Analysis of the Principles of Economics', 1884. Quoted by Kenneth White in his essay 'Looking Out'.

5. George Elder Davie, *The Crisis of the Democratic Intellect*, Edinburgh, Polygon, 1986.

6. In *Stony Limits and Other Poems*, 1934. See *The Complete Poems of Hugh MacDiarmid*, London, Martin Brian & O'Keefe, 1978, vol. 1, p. 422–433.

7. Hugh MacDiarmid, *The Complete Poems*, vol. 2, p. 1271.

8. *On Scottish Ground*, p. 35–48.

9. For example, the chapter 'The Shaman and the Lighthouse-keeper'.

10. First published in a limited edition, with shamanic drawings gathered by White from round the world, as *Le Chemin du chaman*, Lausanne, PAP Édition, 1990. In *Open World*, p. 187–191.

11. The reference here is of course to Robert Graves' study *The White Goddess*, London, Faber and Faber, 1948.

12. First published in 'Pyrenean Meditations', *Atlantica*, p. 43–47. *Open World*, p. 272–278.

13. The essay in question is entitled 'Le paysage archaïque'.

14. Notably, in the essay 'Tam O' Shanter: A New Reading', in *On Scottish Ground*, p. 49–57.

15. Translation by Tony McManus.

16. *Atlantica*, p. 94–105. *The Bird Path*, p. 188–193. *Open World*, p. 515–519.

17. 'A Shaman Dancing on the Glacier', in *On Scottish Ground*, p. 35–48.

18. Introduction to *Le Plateau de l'albatros*. The essays and notes by Kenneth White on language would require a study in itself.

19. Wallace Stevens, *Opus Posthumous*, New York, Vintage Books, 1982.

20. See the chapter 'Sounds', in *Walden*.

21. From White's original English manuscript.

22. Michael Tucker, *Dreaming with Open Eyes – The Shamanic Spirit in Twentieth Century Art and Culture*, San Francisco, Aquarian/Jarper, 1992, p. 183. See also p. 198–202.

23. See the essay 'Scotland, History and the Writer', in *On Scottish Ground*, p. 148–164.

24. *Ibid.*, p. 157.

25. *Ibid.*, p. 158.

26. See White's introduction to his translation of André Breton's *Ode to Charles Fourier*, London, Cape Goliard Press, 1969. The two following quotations are from this text.

27. Norman Bissell, in his Introduction to the book of interviews by Kenneth White with various people in Scotland and France, *Coast to Coast*, p. 9.

28. *Jargon Paper 2*. The *Jargon Papers* have not been taken up by

White in an English-language book so far. They have to be consulted at the Kenneth White archives in Edinburgh (National Library) or in Bordeaux (Bibliothèque Municipale). Translated into French, they figure in the section 'La révolution culturelle à Glasgow', in *Une stratégie paradoxale*.

29. This is from the text 'Essays and Experiments' published by White in the first number of the post-68 review he published in Paris, *The Feathered Egg*. Again, to be consulted in the archives.

30. *Coast to Coast*, p. 112.

31. *The Outsiders – Alexander Trocchi and Kenneth White*, Kirkcaldy, *Akros*, 'Scot View Essays', 1998. The text contains several inaccuracies. On page 15, bad reading and transcription of White's letter of information (sent on request) result in *our heads* coming across as *on ahead* and *further* coming across as *fun then*. On pages 15 and 16, *Tirelli* should be *Torelli*. Further on (p. 18) it is incorrect to say that White distributed Sigma literature in Glasgow, it was Sigma that distributed White's Glasgow texts. Likewise, it is incorrect to say (p. 32) that in the eighties White virtually abandoned verse poetry and waybooks. As to the statement (p. 36) that *the Aquitaine group has a Kenneth White archive*, that also is incorrect – the archive is at the City Library of Bordeaux.

32. *Les Limbes incandescents*, p. 158. Quoted from White's original English manuscript.

33. *The Bird Path*, p. 106–109. *Open World*, p. 279–282.

34. Whitman's poem 'Our Old Feuillage' belongs to that batch of poems in *Leaves of Grass* that contains also 'Salut au Monde', 'Song of the Open Road', 'Crossing Brooklyn Ferry', 'Song of the Answerer', which White considers

the central nucleus of his work.

35. White's editorial in *Feuillage*, n° 1, Pau, January 1968.

36. *The Blue Road*, p. 64–65.

37. 'Scotland, History and the Writer', *On Scottish Ground*, p. 159.

38. 'The Fronting Shore', *On Scottish Ground*, p. 205.

39. 'The Big Rain at Tigh Geal', *Travels in the Drifting Dawn*, p. 134.

40. 'Night in Barcelona', *Travels in the Drifting Dawn*, p. 125.

41. Cioran's *Traité de décomposition* appeared in Paris (Éditions Gallimard) in 1940. It bears as epigraph, this, from Shakespeare's *Richard III*: 'I'll join with black despair against my soul, and to myself become an enemy.' White's *Les Limbes incandescents* has among its epigraphs this quotation from Cioran: 'The offspring of some unfortunate tribe, he walks the boulevards of the West.'

42. Those he was working on at this time went into the books *La Figure du dehors* and *Une apocalypse tranquille*. A fuller map still came with *L'Esprit nomade*. Until the field of geopoetics opened out in *Le Plateau de l'albatros*.

43. 'In the Floating World', *Pilgrim of the Void*, p. 21.

44. *Les Limbes incandescents*, p. 137. Quoted from White's original English manuscript.

45. *Ibid.* p. 51.

46. Gary Snyder, *Earth House Hold*. Quoted p. 34 of White's essay on Snyder, *The Tribal Dharma*.

47. *Le Chant du grand pays*, Nîmes, Terriers, 1989. Translation by Tony McManus.

48. 'Scotland, Intelligence and Culture', *On Scottish Ground*, p. 90.

49. 'Xenophanes of Kolophon', *Handbook for the Diamond Country*, p. 81.

50. In conversation.

51. The No play is the *Suma Genji*.

52. 'Last Page of a Notebook', *Handbook for the Diamond Country*, p. 76.

53. 'The Region of Identity', *The Bird Path*, p. 97–100. *Open World*, p. 202.

54. 'Hölderlin in Bordeaux', *The Bird Path*, p. 91–93. *Open World*, p. 287–288.

55. 'A High Blue Day on Scalpay', *Handbook for the Diamond Country*, p. 77. *Open World*, p. 98.

56. *The Works of Ralph Waldo Emerson*, London, George Bell and Sons, 1907.

57. Preface to the 1855 edition of *Leaves of Grass*.

58. Charles Olson, *Human Universe*, New York, Grove Press, 1967, p. 19.

59. This volume has not yet been published.

60. T. S. Eliot, *Collected Poems* 1909–1935.

61. Preface to *Pilgrim of the Void*, p. 12.

62. In conversation with the author.

63. *Pilgrim of the Void*, p. 12.

64. 'A Fragment of Yellow Silk', in *Handbook for the Diamond Country*, p. 114. *Open World*, p. 308.

65. 'Meditant', *Handbook for the Diamond Country*, p. 185. *Open World*, p. 456.

66. He uses it, for example, as epigraph for his poem 'Interpetations of a Twisted Pine', in *The Bird Path*, p. 79. *Open World*, p. 213.

67. Quoted by Nobuyuki Yusa in his Introduction to his translation of Basho's *The Narrow Road to the Deep North and Other Travel Sketches*, Harmondsworth, Penguin Books, 1966, p. 33.

68. This development by Suzuki, as well as the following references and quotations, is to be found in D. T. Suzuki, Erich Fromm and Richard De Martino, *Zen Buddhism and Psychoanalysis*, New York, Harper and Row, 1960.

69. See *The Ten Principal Upanishads* put into English by Shree Purohit Swâmi and W. B. Yeats, London, Faber and Faber, 1937.

70. See the poem 'A Coat', in W. B. Yeats, *Selected Poetry*, London, Macmillan & Co, 1962.

71. See Fenollosa and Ezra Pound, *The Chinese Written Character as a Medium for Poetry*, San Francisco, City Lights Books, 1969 (fifth printing).

72. These are fragments from the final stages of Pound's Canto work.

73. See the poem 'Finisterra, or the Logic of Lannion Bay', in the bilingual *Les Rives du silence. Open World*, p. 575. Significant here too is that, in the field of geopoetics, White will never use the term 'geopoet', but always 'geopoetician' – like logician, or mathematician.

74. Karl Popper, *The Logic of Scientific Discovery*, London, Routledge, 1934.

75. Specific references can be found here and there. For example, in *Les Limbes incandescents* (p. 52), where there is this quotation from Dirac's *Quantum Mechanics*: 'A profound change has taken place during the present century in the opinions physicists have held as to the mathematical foundations of their subject.

[. . .] Quantum mechanics provides a good example of the new ideas. It requires the states of a dynamical system and the dynamical variables to be interconnected in quite strange ways that are unintelligible from the classical standpoint.' (Quoted from White's original English manuscript.) Passing references apart, what is important are the general conclusions (and confirmations) that White took from these mathematics and physics.

76. 'Theory', *Handbook for the Diamond Country*, p. 108. *Open World*, p. 609.

77. 'Time on a Dark River', in *Travels in the Drifting Dawn*, p. 22.

78. The graphics, indeed the seismography, of this movement is one of the lines that White follows in his essays.

79. The Encyclopedists, it will be remembered, were part of White's teaching at Glasgow, and elsewhere.

80. This was an intermediary stage on the way to geopoetics, which contains all the scope and energies of the former term, but in a more 'nuclear', condensed manner.

81. 'Scotland, Intelligence and Culture', in *On Scottish Ground*, p. 86–94.

82. The first book on catastrophe theory he studied was Thom's *Modèles mathématiques de la morphogenèse*, Paris, Union Générale d'Édition, 1974. This was followed by Thom's interviews on mathematics, science and philosophy (moving into geomorphology and tectonics) entitled *Paraboles et catastrophes*, Paris, Flammarion, 1980.

83. 'The Fronting Shore', *On Scottish Ground*, p. 202–219.

84. This and the following three quotations are from the English translation by White of an essay that appeared first, in French, as 'Un journal de bord du Pacifique', in *L'Esprit*

nomade, p. 305–314. What White does in this essay is to extract the logic of the logbook and develop it. Taken up again in *The Wanderer and his Charts*, p. 66–73, as 'Reflections on a Logbook'.

85. First published in English in the review *Les Langues modernes*, Paris, janvier–février 1966. Taken up later, in French, as 'L'Université bidon', in *Une stratégie paradoxale*.

86. This is from a sheet distributed hand to hand in May '68, entitled 'Cri sur l'université'.

87. This is from an essay entitled 'Towards a Creative University', first published, in English, in n° 5 (May, 1969) of the review White started up in Pau, *Feuillage*, thereafter in n° 2 (January, 1973) of the review he started up in Paris, *The Feathered Egg*. Taken up later, in French, as 'Vers une université créatrice', in *Une stratégie paradoxale*.

88. Published in French as 'Les origines de l'université bourgeoise en France', in *Feuillage*, n° 5 (May, 1969).

89. See George Davie, *The Democratic Intellect*, Edinburgh U. P., 1961.

90. Quoted in George Davie, *op. cit.*, p. 127.

91. Interview, 'A New Energy Field', in *Coast to Coast*, p. 103–116. As for the two quotations in the following paragraph.

92. Interview, 'From the Centred Complex', *Coast to Coast*, p. 117–126.

93. Breton made this statement in a text 'Braise au trépied de Keridwen', that served as preface to a translation of old Welsh Poems, *Les Grands bardes gallois*, Paris, Falaize, 1956. White quotes it in his essay 'Paysage physique, paysage mental', in the review *Incisions III, op. cit.*

94. *Ibid.*

95. *Écosse*, Paris, Éditions Arthaud, 1984, p. 7 and 9.

96. 'Scotia Deserta', *The Bird Path*, p. 123–127. *Open World*, p. 598–602.

97. 'Labrador', *The Bird Path*, p. 181–186. *Open World*, p. 520–525.

98. This is a multi-layered complex concept which no mere quibbling about White's own name will get anywhere near. For a quick summary of its meanings, see the interview, 'Following out World Lines', in *Coast to Coast*, p. 65–86.

99. The reference here is to Renan's essay, 'The Poetry of the Celtic Races'. White read it first in the book of Renan's essays published by the Walter Scott Publishing Co, London and Felling-on-Tyne, 1896, which he bought as a student from a book-barrow in Glasgow. While appreciating some of its formulae, he soon saw its shortcomings: its 'celtism' too narrow and nostalgic – and White himself never talks of 'race', but of language, thought and landscape. Years later, in Brittany, White did a thorough reading, discriminating and critical, but also reinvigorating and renovative, of Renan's complete works. See 'Un goût vif de l'univers', in *Le Plateau de l'albatros*.

100. This is a phrase often quoted by White.

101. White also likes to quote another of the insults Jerome threw at Pelagius: 'Heavy with Scotch porridge' (*Scotis pultibus praegravatus*).

102. See White's translation of this poem, London, Cape Goliard Press, 1969.

PART THREE:
OPEN WORLD WRITING

I'm thinking of a writing knowing how to move through local systems and sensitive fields towards world-logic and world-sensation.

KENNETH WHITE,
On Scottish Ground

White works in three forms of literary expression. His prose narrative 'waybooks' follow a narrative figure out of the contemporary Western context through the cultures of the earth and into its empty spaces where he is imbued with a 'sense of world' – a clarification of perception in relation to the earth itself. The essays chart a similar movement in a more analytical form. The poetry is of two kinds. The long poems White refers to as 'peregrinations' in the spaces of the earth and the mind. The short 'diamond' poems evoke intense moments of perception. The three forms overlap considerably: analytical passages are found in the 'waybooks', which are also interspersed with poems; the poems can be long analyses of ideas or significant cultural figures; the essays reach moments of poem-like imagery and focus.

In White's mind, there is no precedence or hierarchy among these three forms. If, chronologically, he began with the poem, moved from there to the less intense but more inclusive form of prose narrative, and from there went on to the essay, the logic of the complete work is triple.

White has likened this triple writing activity to an arrow: the feathers representing the essays, giving direction; the shaft of the arrow being the books of ongoing biography, the waybooks; and the point of the arrow being the poem. Using another image, he'll say the essays are cartography; the narrative books are exploration of particular landscapes, territorial itineraries; and the poems, condensations of travel, or particularly enlightened moments along the itineraries.

1. The Essay

White has said that one of the first texts that got him interested in literature was R. L. Stevenson's book of essays, *Men and Books*[1]. Why? Principally there's the fact of Stevenson describing himself pleasantly as 'a literary vagrant', a fact illustrated by the scope of the essays, which range from Anglo-American literature (Whitman, Thoreau) to Far-Eastern culture (the Japanese Yoshida Torajiro), via French literature (François Villon, Victor Hugo). At the same time, there's a difference. Stevenson himself says, charmingly, disarmingly, in his Introduction that he is well aware of the overpersonal nature of his essays, not necessarily superficial, but based on a momentary point of view which could very well vary at some other moment, since none of the essays are based on a fundamental study of the context involved.

While he enjoys their work (in a cursory kind of way), this is a lack White finds in most English language essayists, which is why he includes them in the category of 'Belles-Lettres' rather than in that of cogent essay-writing.

Among the essayists White has found pleasant, but fundamentally wanting, the Charles Lambs, the Leigh Hunts, the Oliver Goldsmiths, one can single out William Hazlitt, not only because he has White's preference ('On Going a Journey' was a favourite with the adolescent White), but because Hazlitt has some remarks on style which singularly attracted him. Here's Hazlitt on what he calls 'the familiar style' in the essay with that title:

It is not easy to write a familiar style. Many people mistake a familiar for a vulgar style, and suppose that to write without affectation is to write at random. On the contrary, there is nothing that requires more precision, and, if I may say so, purity of expression, than the style I am speaking of.

There's a lot of White's style in those remarks: the avoidance of heaviness, the breaking out of respectable norms, a free-swinging movement, with at the same time an extreme care for precision, exactness, clarity.

Among English-language essayists, the early Americans constituted for White a class apart, precisely because they were more concerned with *context* than their British counterparts. White did not look to Emerson for style, finding him often ponderous and diffuse, but he did look to him, as we've seen, for the content of essays such as 'The American Scholar', 'The Progress of Culture', 'Society and Solitude'. The same could be said of the essays of Thoreau (much more interesting to White as a stylist) such as 'Life without Principle', and of those of Whitman: 'Democratic Vistas', 'The Death of Thomas Carlyle', and, of course, the Preface to the 1855 edition of *Leaves of Grass*. With these works, White was in his element. These were essayists not concerned simply with 'fine literature', but with trying out (essaying) a ground.

The only 'Anglo-Saxon' essayist of modern times with anything like that urgency and tendency was D. H. Lawrence. But if White appreciated Lawrence at the time of his early researches, even then he did not share the almost hysterical urgency of Lawrence, and loathed both the 'repetitive rhetoric'[2] of the Englishman, and the 'horribly chatty' nature of his style.

It's to France one must look for the source of important elements in White's essay work.

It will be remembered that Kenneth White's decision to leave Britain for France in 1967 was partly prompted by his publisher's wary attitude, expressed in a recommendation to write social-realist fiction, to the increasingly radical nature of his work.

White's instinct that the context that would nurture his work was in France was, then, quickly and authoritatively confirmed. There, people like Breton, Artaud, Bachelard, Deleuze, Guattari, Michaux . . . had been busy deconstructing (before the word was ever upper-cased) the politico-religious and psycho-analytical foundations of modernism – genuinely radical work without its counterpart on any comparable scale in the 'Anglo-Saxon' countries.

In his essays – most still not published in English – White explores the writers mentioned above as well as others referred to earlier, minds engaged on the 'deep path', such as the quantum theorists who debunked the illusion of subject-object and space-time dualisms, the fractal geometricians who place energy and matter at the heart of our analytical thinking, their linguistic-poetic counterparts such as Fenollosa and the philosophers like Husserl and Heidegger who reground 'being' in the experience of and presence in the world. In these contexts, which dismantle Platonic idealism and Aristotelian categorisation, the word 'radical' has to be understood as referring to work (and living) which puts in question the ideological foundations of the West and the modern developments of these – humanism, rationalism, dualism (the separating of body from mind, and the human from the earth), which diminish the outlook of human minds from a cosmological perspective (the domain of poetics), to the constrictions of the social and the psychological (the domain of fiction).

In an essay entitled 'Aquitanian Affinities'[3], White speaks about his relationship to Europe's original essayist, Michel de Montaigne.

Montaigne's essays, which he describes as 'a register of my attempts (essays) at living', cover a wide range of existential themes, from imagination to philosophy, from daily living to ethnology, from education to politics, and from there to the pleasures of solitude. Beyond the thematics, it's the figure of the solitary thinker that first attracted White, seeing Montaigne there in his tower-library in Aquitaine as he was later to see Spinoza in his workroom at Rhynnsberg, or Nietzsche in his room on the Engadine plateau: individuals trying to get at all the dimensions, all the co-ordinates, of a full existence.

Stylistically, Montaigne's dictum was: 'On the paper as in the mouth', which is to say that he wanted to keep an oral force in his writing. But, more precisely, what kind of orality? In one of his essays[4], he has this: 'Above us, up there towards the mountains, there's a Gascon language I find singularly sharp, fine and full of meaning.' Elsewhere, and it fills out the description, he'll speak of 'a muscular, succulent language', and of a style that is 'brusque and powerful' rather than 'delicate and polished'; what this meant was, not a return to ethnic dialect (Montaigne is very explicit on this), but the desire, the determination to maintain a certain 'barbarousness' in his French. This is what White does with his English.

Compared thematically with Montaigne, White is less

concerned with self-portrait than with a field of energy, maybe a cosmography. His essays are devoted to his own explorations in this cosmographic field, moving, say, from a consideration of granite on the coast of Scotland or Brittany to magnetic polarity, philosophy East and West and poetics of the world. He has followed many paths, has left himself open to many influences, crossed many fields and territories. But if all the elements and energies, forces and forms that can be listed with regard to this work are aligned, they must be seen as tributaries to a river that takes them all in and, most importantly, moves them ever onwards.

2. The Waybook

White's prose-narrative books combine these mental investigations with geographical exploration of various territories and terrains.

In *Pilgrim of the Void*, he is paying one of his frequent visits to the market place, this time in Bangkok, when he comes across a sign of the radical vision and its non-radical counterpart. A fish falls off its slab and *flip flops its way along a drier and drier path*. It reminds him of the oceanic origins of life and leads him to contemplate the different degrees of awareness of these signs in Oriental and Occidental culture:

It's this consciousness that the real problem of man is

that of being a fish-out-of-water that you find in the East. The West tends to have a shorter memory, and to get worked up about secondary and absurd issues like how a lot of half-dead fish are going to be able to live together and get to Heaven. The East, the old East, is concerned about how to get back to the ocean, or to find some substitute for it.[5]

In the West, the word 'radical' is too often applied to what is little more than the more energetic thrashings of those half-dead fish, flapping and choking in the nets of personal identity and religious-political expectation. As asforesaid:

> The whole of Western civilisation is a compound of expectations whether it be for the Messiah, the Future or God knows what all else. Even when it's given up waiting for anything else, doesn't it keep waiting for Godot?[6]

Concerning the real radical ground, the novel, the written expression of that constricted modern outlook, is no longer adequate to the task. Kenneth White's prose-narrative books reflect new radical movement and embody a new form of literary expression.

Travels in the Drifting Dawn, The Blue Road, and *Pilgrim of the Void* are definitely 'waybooks', that is books in which a narrative 'I' is voyaging in a given earth-space and in a developing mind-space. While a similar way is being travelled in *Incandescent Limbo, Letters from Gourgounel* and *House of Tides*, the physical experience is more of a *residence* than an *errancy* as the narrative voice moves around seven rooms in Paris, or settles into an abandoned Ardèche farm, or muses on the house and seascape of the author's Breton home since 1983. Always the subject is ultimately about human dwelling on the earth. Etymologically, the word 'dwelling' includes the notion of 'delay' and therefore implies 'movement' – the idea of 'dwelling' is as a moment in the nomadic journey, a moment of repose and of concentration of energies and resources gathered for the journey to come. A moment which might be an hour, days, a season, years, generations even of settled existence before the wandering begins again. It is the story of human history if looked at from far enough up to see beyond the narrow historical parameters of our normal mentality.

The books take off from an autobiographical departure point – all the journeys and residencies and their events and experiences are real, the imaginative enterprise involved is one of composition. Given the untrammelled tone of much of this work, it may come as a surprise to know that some years go into the condensing of the gathered material. *Incandescent Limbo*, in fact, was only published in book form after twelve years of work on the composition of its various elements. Despite this 'artifice', the books are quite lacking in that feeling of manipulation, that sense of something being 'set up' which so few novelists have ever been able to separate from 'plot'. And the prose retains a freshness and vigour, a rhythm which has, at times, the allure of a man out walking in the world:

> Clear Autumn along the Gassan trail, torrent tumbling ridge to ridge, crows cawing, North wind blowing, one foot after another, breathing three to three, haiku-walking . . .[7]

An autobiographical starting-point means a socio-personal

context, which, in turn, means that elements of the fiction-writer's craft are still present in these books. I am thinking of the skaters on the pond (a real nineteenth century novelist's vignette!) in *Incandescent Limbo*. Or the deft and vivid character portrayals of the villagers in *Letters from Gourgounel* – Monsieur Martin the postman, 'a walking wine-sack' or Mme Teston with her refrain: 'it's finished here, the good times are finished'. I'm thinking also of the evocation of the teeming city in the various countries of *Travels in the Drifting Dawn*, and of the little towns of Brittany in *House of Tides*. Also the socio-political commentary which is subtly, but pointedly, present in the exposition of military and economic exploitation in *Pilgrim of the Void*, and strongly overt in the lambasting of religious and colonialist devastation of the Amerindian peoples in *The Blue Road*. This is the (radical) voice of an Algonquin:

> . . . if you can make any sense at all out of what the Jesuits try to put down our throats, I'll be very grateful to you. But, if you yourself believe what they believe, we may as well call a halt right now. For they've told us such an ill pack of nonsense that I can hardly do them the intellectual insult of believing they believe it all themselves . . .[8]

The narrator who is living these experiences starts off with the recognisable attributes of a fictional protagonist. He has a name, Kenneth White, and comes from Scotland. He has memories which come into play in the scenes through which he passes, in particular memories of his father – a railway signalman, their home village of Fairlie, student years in Glasgow, stravaiging in the land and seascapes of the west coast. Even when, for convenience in the East, he says 'yes' to the inevitable question, 'American?', or says he is French to enquirers in *The Blue Road*, it does not serve only to destabilise notions of personal identity, it also, paradoxically, serves to confirm them. In *The Blue Road*, the narrator of the opening pages is quite clearly a created fictive persona – still Kenneth White, yet in a naive-jocose mode which is designed to offset the enclosed mentality of a certain urban context in Montreal. It is a protagonist who, in the earlier books, is experiencing a profound crisis and even 'moments of panic', moments when language becomes fervid and dislocated, one main image of this perhaps being the gathering storm throughout *Letters from Gourgounel*.

The social and personal contexts are not, then, totally discarded, on the contrary they are fully participated in, and expressed with the insight and craft of the fictional master.

But there is more to this narrator than that. That fictive persona of the opening of *The Blue Road* resurfaces later in the book in mytho-fabulous form as Carcajou, the wolverine and Trickster, and when White says of the colonialist encounter with the native Americans:

> The Indian gradually gets pushed to the side. The intruder has become the inhabitant, and the inhabitant becomes the outcast.[9]

he is also creating an image, linking exterior and interior realities, of the Western mind full of philosophical, political 'intrusions' which have pushed the Indian in us, the earth-grounded awareness, to one side. The narrator is on the search for this archaic ground on which to rebuild his being. As he says in *Incandescent Limbo*, watching the skaters:

> . . . I stand there observing, like a novelist, but I tire of
> this pretty quickly, and move away on my own into the ice-
> gripped woods.[10]

For one thing, this is not only a body participating in a series
of incidents, this is also a mind which sets out on its journeys
having studied the geology, the anthropology, the history,
geography, languages and literature of the places it passes
through. It is a mind which takes time out from narrative to
make lengthy commentaries, disrupting the normal narrative
flow, on Taoist and Mahayana texts or the lives and writings of
other intellectual nomad figures who have passed on similar
paths before, or the Inuit and Ainu shaman-poetry of Labrador
and Hokkaido (remarkably 'contemporary' in their clear, fresh
feel). When this body-mind journeys through a Parisian quarter
– a yellow-black reminiscence of Baudelaire – towards the Seine
and writes:

> I go down to the river, to its cold non-being, beyond the
> shadows and the reflections, that chill non-being, distant.[11]

the universal scope of the mind and its references makes you
think not only 'Seine'[12], but also, 'Ganges'. And when he writes in
Letters from Gourgounel:

> The entire valley, with its chestnut trees in the rain, is
> blue-green; above: grey sky and mist in the mountain.[13]

the Chinese feel is so strong in that book – explicit in its references, its chapters on translation of Chinese poetry, implicit in its brilliantly sympathetic yet detached tone and its painterly descriptions of landscape – that you sense you are with Li Po or Han Shan in their mountain retreats (that 'blue-green' is the colour of Han Shan's mountain, coincidentally the meaning also of 'Cairngorm'). It is this ability to become *other*, to identify with the landscape and to move across space and time through the power of the contemplating mind, which brings the narrator through that storm, and others like it.

Everywhere he goes, this narrator is looking for signs of an original ground from which thought and expression can start again: primal images with universal significances.

Visiting a buddhist shrine in *Pilgrim*, he goes past it, to the real reason for its presence, a special feature of the landscape, a waterfall beside the kiosk. That is the true 'buddha': 'This isn't even China any more. It's just water falling into water.' In *The Blue Road*, he meets an Indian woman with a 'funny little squashed bonnet, sausage ringlets at her ears and a pipe in her mouth', and realises he is looking at the same person he met among the Meo people of Thailand and whom he will meet again, in signs here and there. Her ancestors had:

> wandered north and kept wandering (what were they really hunting for?) and finally crossed the Bering Straits (can you hear the wolves howling under that frozen moon, can you hear the ice cracking?) and became American.[14]

That image reflects the movement of White's writing, unlike the archetypal Western prose-narrative which starts with a panoramic view of the landscape as background, then moves, slowly, to the 'human drama' which is played out there with occasional symbolic-nostalgic reference back to the landscape for 'poetic effect'. That is a modern (that is, post-seventeenth century) movement from geography to history, from myth to fiction, from cosmological possibility to socio-psychological definition. It is characterised by a loss of energy and a narrowing of perception transmuted into a fateful nostalgia. Lewis Grassic Gibbon's *A Scots Quair*[15], for all its beautiful and moving moments, would fit such a description. Kenneth White's prose narratives work in the opposite direction. They *start* in the congested social context – which is not without sympathy, life and humour, or indeed signs of something more fully alive, but which is, finally, restricting. They move from there into space and light, places of breathing and seeing and a sense of being centred in the world as opposed to being the centre *of* the world. It is a movement away from contexts which define, that is, *limit* one as a 'personality', to open and illuminating spaces where, losing all such prescriptive definitions, the human being becomes conscious of being *in relationship with*, rather than *as distinct from*, nature. It is a movement which White has described in relation to the Japanese artist, Hokusai, in a remarkable book on him written in French and published in France, towards:

> the intuition of a point of observation situated at such a considerable height, that his vision, while not losing contact with the most immediate details, would be almost limitless.[16]

So we move from the crowded streets of Hong Kong and Bangkok, the departure lounge at Charles de Gaulle Airport, or a fast-food bar in Montreal, out in a northerly direction, towards great earth-spaces – as with the gathering of wild Siberian swans in Hokkaido, or in the Bay of Ungava, or in the mountains of Mae Sai:

> Before me, blue woven into blue, is Burma: hills, a river, a village, a temple. I take these elements, work through them: the temple, the village, the river, the hills, the curves, the blue, the blue energy, the pulsions . . . All pulsant blue: moving silence, mobile immobility.[17]

In that use of blue, in that word 'pulsant', in the 'weaving' of abstract and concrete, the detailed vision of the landscape becomes, at the same time, a cosmic perception evoking the energy and forms of the world.

Undeniably, the perspective is so large, the aim so big and the crystal-like effect of different styles of writing and tone within the one text so delicate that the tensions which exist between these can come close now and then to mannerism, more pronounced in the first attempt at this style of book *Travels in the Drifting Dawn*. The retention of the socio-personal context, and the return to it at the end of *The Blue Road* and *Pilgrim of the Void*, seem designed to stop any drift into esotericism, to point to the possible function of the enlightened mind back within the social context.

Generally, there is nothing heavy or forced about these correspondences, they seem to establish themselves naturally in the course of the writing. This is because the writing, and this is true of White's poetry as it is of his prose narratives, makes what Gaston Bachelard[18] calls 'the radical difference between image and metaphor'. For Bachelard, a metaphor is an 'ephemeral expression', 'a false image'. Crucially, 'it does not really unite exterior reality and intimate reality'. That very separation of exterior and intimate makes the metaphor the prime form of expression in Western culture, identified as it is by its Aristotelian separating of reality out into analysable categories. The novel cannot go beyond this separatism without putting its own nature at risk. *Moby Dick*, for example, goes so far into the phenomenon of the white whale it becomes an image and the book ceases to become a novel. In this description of the Camargue in *Travels in the Drifting Dawn*, perceiver and perceived are one as man (the narrator), landscape, expression and the erotic energy of life are united:

> The Camargue is the hieroglyph of a stump of branch projecting above the surface of a marsh, or the ideogram of a skull encrusted in sand. It is the quick excitement of seeing lithe forms in rippling water and the feeling that at any moment you may meet that girl, that woman, 'her smooth legs still bearing the salt of the primal sea . . .'[19]

Much literature and all psychology, in Bachelard's eyes, do not go beyond the *resonances* of experience and its metaphorical expression, while the true image *reverberates* with being, bringing the reader into an intimate relationship with the writer so that we are drawn into his experience and its cosmic reverberations across time and space. Bachelard's name for this poetic experience is 'intimate immensity', a lovely phrase which would apply to the culminating moments of perception in White's waybooks when the socio-personal trappings of the narrator and their fictional expression have been slowly sloughed off till the narrator becomes a contemplating presence within the landscape, part of it. Accompanying this, necessarily, is a honing-down of language to prevent it getting in the way of the 'intimacy' and the 'immensity', freeing it from the convolutions of the metaphor, and leading it to the clarity of the image. It is language which is not elaborated by the writer in order to close us in to his view of reality, but which is made plain and bare in order to open our perception out. The phrase would also apply to the reader's sharing of these moments when you become at one with the narrative spirit.

The main thrust here is to do with a radical shift in living, thought, and expression of which White's waybooks are an important development. It is a shift which is related to the inter-subjectivity of transcendental phenomenology, which itself corresponds to the demise of the subject-object dualism which modern physics demonstrates when it points out that the perceiver participates in the identity of that which is perceived. These moments are the culminating and self-destructive points of Western rationalism, reuniting Western awareness with the theories of identity and energy to be found in the Eastern cerebral hemisphere of, say, White's oft-quoted phrase from the Upanishads' 'you are that', which is to say the same thing as Bachelard says of the image in the quotation above.

Given that implicit in all this is the idea that the reader is participating in these books just as the narrator is at work on the experiences he is recounting, it is difficult to extract illustrative episodes in isolation from the context of the whole book, which has carefully, if unobtrusively, cleared the ground for that culminating experience. However, the culminating episode in *The Wild Swans*, the final section of *Pilgrim of the Void*, is a most striking example of this arrival in a renewed world-space. The narrator sets out for the North Island of Hokkaido with a dream in mind, 'to see the wild swans coming swooping and whooping from Siberia to winter in Japan's northern lakes'. It is a dream which echoes Basho's in *The Narrow Road to the Deep North*: 'I was already dreaming of the full moon rising over the islands of Matsushima.' The narrator journeys from the 'bedlam' of the city, Tokyo, northwards, penetrating more and more into the landscape which he paints for the reader with deft, colourful touches, and into the perceptive culture of Japan and its links with the 'hyperborean' culture with its shamanistic basis. These things take form in our minds through the commentaries and quotations which derive from and lead back into the landscape. At the end the narrator has become a kind of presence, of which we seem, uncannily, a part, waiting on a lake in the Bay of Natsuke until:

> . . . on the evening of the fifth day's waiting, with twilight coming down blue and rose, there was a great cry in the air, a great
>
> *whoo*　　　　　　*whoo*　　　　　　*whoo*
>
> and then a rushing sound of wings [. . .]
> Suddenly the emptiness was full of clamour and beating wings.
> They came in groups of five to ten.
> First one group.
> Then another.
> Then another.
> I waited till there were about ninety birds on the lake, then went to the inn to sleep, intending to be up before dawn.[20]

In a book which has been criticised for one or two steamy encounters in Bangkok, this is the most erotically charged moment. The passage truly 'reverberates'. The astute choice and placing of colour, the myth-like construction of 'on the evening of the fifth day', the ecstatic (and humorous) onomatopoeia of the swans' cry, and, above all, the sexual rhythm of the sentences echoing the erotic rhythm of the swans, create a perception so truly lived and expressed that the reader becomes a co-participant in the perception, enters into the landscape and the event along with the narrator.

The literary form White has evolved to express these movements has its precedents which, as one might expect, range widely across time and space. The idea of 'pilgrim' may evoke for us Lourdes and Mecca, at best Chaucer and John Bunyan, but in the Eastern tradition the 'pilgrim' is the key figure, the 'way' the central theme. At a conference in France in 1988[21], White traced this lineage, quoting the Indian writer Ananda Coomaraswamy in *The Way of the Pilgrim*:

> Pilgrimage is a process which consists in going from potentiality to act, from non-being to being, from obscurity to light.

In Chinese Taoist literature, White reminds us in his essay, the answer to the question, 'what is the Tao?' is 'Go!'. In the interesting fringes of Islam, there is the waybook of the Saliq, 'the wearer of blue' (which colour permeates White's work like the distinctive blue of Hokusai's paintings), who passes by the North to find enlightenment. In America, the Indian awareness which informs the most outward-looking literature was

177

awakened by Black Elk's comment on the Amerindian culture which had been eliminated at Wounded Knee. One day, he thought, 'people may once more find the good red road.' It was this sentiment which informed the road-books of the Beats, but more rigorous predecessors in America are Whitman, Thoreau in his residence at Walden Pond or in his travels to the Maine Woods and Cape Cod. Coming closer to home, if further out in time, the Celtic monks who wandered through Europe also provide, to a greater or lesser extent, existential and intellectual antecedents for this work.

But it is Basho of whom White is the true heir in these books, and not just in respect of following in his footsteps in his celebrated journey to 'the deep north' (to which he adds a sensual element often missing in the Japanese work). Basho, in his time, revitalised a long tradition of road literature, the *mishiyuki-bun*, and thereby re-energised Japanese poetry. His poem about the true inflection of poetry heard for the first time in 'the rice-planting songs of the far north' echoes the much earlier Chinese poet, Wang Wei (701–761) who is the subject of a chapter in *Letters from Gourgounel* and whose 'Response to the Magistrate Chang' was:

> Ultimate reality?
> – the song of the fisherman off among the reeds.

As White points out, Basho's *The Narrow Road to the Deep North* represented a radical transformation of Japanese prose in achieving a brilliantly fluent linking of poetry and prose, of narrative and discourse, of the past (through the citation of previous writers, thinkers and historical figures) and the present.

And he achieved, after long searching, in the haiku moments of these prose books, an expression of deeply concentrated and yet limitlessly expansive light. White's waybooks achieve a similarly fluent linking of diverse forms, attitudes, feelings and ideas, all united in a beautiful evocation of the earth which re-establishes a 'sense of *world*'.

Speaking of Hokusai, he could be speaking of his own prose narrative work:

> These are scenes of the void and the wind, and of that whiteness which, according to Chuang Tzu, 'surges up from the house of the void', scenes from which, through line and colour, a powerful poetry arises, a poetics of the open world.[22]

3. The Poem of the Earth

White has said with humour that if his grandfather was a musician (a piper), if his uncle played the saxophone in jazz bands, if his father could get a good tune out of a mouth organ, he himself played and plays no instrument. But that the work of this writer and poet contains a great deal of music (not, certainly, of a classical type), there is no doubt. White has gone into his musical affinities (Erik Satie, Busoni, John Cage, Glenn Gould . . .) in an essay[23] in his introduction to geopoetics, *Le Plateau de l'albatros*. Here I want to go into the question from another angle.

In Walden, it will be remembered[24], Thoreau talks about an owl making 'such a sound as the frozen earth would make if struck with a suitable plectrum', and of the thrill he got from hearing a cat-owl calling out to a flight of honking geese:

> It was one of the most thrilling discords I ever heard. And yet, if you had a discriminating ear, there were in it the elements of a concord such as these plains never saw or heard.

We've also seen White (in whose poems, and prose texts, onomatopoeic bird-calls abound) talking in general terms about a 'listening in to nature'. Here he is 'listening in' to 'the music of the landscape'[25]:

> *Listening in*
> *(late August morning)*
> *to the music of the landscape:*
> *sea-wind*
> *blowing veil after veil of grey*
> *up the valley of Goaslagorn*
> *flights of wailing birds*
> *over the fields*
> *young birches*
> *with scarcely frosted trunks*
> *rain-whispering*
> *hoarse ragged firtrees on the skyline . . .*
> *along the shore*
> *(all the islands wrapped in mist*
> *but the surf outlines them*
> *with silent thunder)*
> *a restlessness, a movingness*

a chaos-noisiness:
unruled masses of sound
interrupted by sharp cries
or a wave breaking
on ice-scored rock
(no place this for
sympathies or symphonies
any kind of easy
harmonisation:
the weather is everchanging
and from Dourven point
to Ploumanac'h's centred complex
the topography abrupt) –
yet there is
something like a music there
in the grey rain
and the sharp cries
and the wind
that travels the changing skies
there is something immensely
satisfying to the mind
corresponding
to its highest demand:
admitting no simple equations
and laughing at any solemn questions.

Anyone with a discriminating ear knows there is 'something like a music' there.

Now, if White's poetic music has affinities to some of the most recent developments in instrumental music, it could be also that, intuitively, he is tuning in also on very ancient tradition.

In his *Scotland's Music*[26], John Purser gives a neat demonstration of how the musical language of the Scottish

Gaeltachdt takes its form from the landscape, using as an
example the song of the redshank whose life on the
discontinuities of sea and land which is the shore is analogous to,
perhaps in a sense identified with, the discontinuity which is the
subject of keening – a death in the community. In a radio
programme on the subject, a Hebridean woman sings her
versions of the calls of the puffin, razorbill and guillemot and
when Purser plays recordings of the birds themselves afterwards,
he explains a difference between human song and original bird
song with what might seem a ludicrous comment:

> The relationships of the calls with the human imitation
> is not as close as in the other recordings; but one must also
> allow for the individual experience of the human who may
> have heard birds with different regional accents than those
> on the recording.

'Birds with different regional accents'! But if the human
voice as is suggested by the first extract takes its intonations,
pitches and rhythms from the landscape, then why not the other
animals who share the air, climate, the seasonal changes, the
sounds, sights and smells of that landscape? Perhaps we may find
the idea ridiculous because we no longer listen as those Gaelic
women listened. And if not, why not? What has happened to us?
Here is Kenneth White on the subject of 'the pure music of the
landscape':

> What is sure is that with the installation of civilisation
> we listen to it no longer. The civilised person listens to the
> politicians, listens to fabricated music, listens to himself. It
> is only at the end of civilisations that certain individuals,
> solitary types, isolated, start again to listen to the

landscape.[27]

We have been for some time at the end of 'civilisation'. What White attempts to do is not to see 'doomsday' in such an end, but the beginning of something else which will involve, to some extent, the return to things we left behind some time ago. It is the opportunity for what White calls in the title of one of his essay books, *A Quiet Apocalypse*[28], an apocalypse that is the prelude to *Le Plateau de l'albatros*[29] (the title of White's book on geopoetics).

White's nomadising in the byways of culture leads him to the conclusion that instead of attempting to understand the human in relation to itself, we must perceive the human in relation to the earth, that is develop that 'sense of world' whose felt loss has been the spur of all his work. This is the 'geo' in 'geopoetics'. The 'poetics' covers the realisation, also derived from that nomadising, that when the human being hits upon genuine perception of reality, the desire to express that perception is part of it:

> Geopoetics is concerned with 'worlding' (and 'wording' is contained in 'worlding'). In my semantics, 'world' emerges from a contact between the human mind and the things, the lines, the rhythms of the earth, the person in relation to the planet. When this contact is sensitive, subtle, intelligent, you have 'a world' (a culture) in the strong, confirming and enlightening sense of the word. When that contact is insensitive, simplistic and stupid, you don't have a world at all, you have a non-world, a pseudo-culture, a dictatorial enclosure or a mass-mess. Geopoetics is concerned with developing sensitive and intelligent contact, and with working out original ways to express that contact.[30]

For White, poetics is a fundamental word, underlying science, literature, philosophy, and coordinating elements arising from all these disciplines. Because the 'normal' condition of man is artificial, so is his language. Therefore, the geopoetic poem seeks a new form of expression. This leads to a radically different approach to the form of poetry than is the norm in the English canon. For White, the language of poetry must reveal the world. Poetry as we are accustomed to it in the English canon rarely reveals world. We are offered an artefact constructed of metaphors, metrics, word and sound-play, often beautifully made, but only revealing the poet. Poetry which reveals a world will not point back in on itself like this, rather it will be, to use Gaston Bachelard's memorable description, 'the flare-up of being in the imagination'[31]. White's writing is full of such incandescent moments as that evoked by Bachelard's phrase as in this from 'In the Sea and Pine Country'[32]:

> *an occasional cry*
> *enlarges the silence*

Here, the great silence which is the poet's experience of the world at a moment of high perceptiveness is, paradoxically, brought to greater realisation by the single cry of a bird within it. This image pares the poet's experience down to the essential sign and simplest language, but it has the opposite effect on the reader whose mind is filled, from this starting point, with the 'sense of world' which has inspired the lines. And the lines themselves reflect the poetic practice being pointed to – it's the small 'cry' of the poet which indicates the vast 'sense of world'.

So much Western poetry (and this is as true of modern poetry as it is of its precedents) invites you to look with the eyes of the particular poet concerned. The poet's ego, personality, 'self', call it what you will, is mostly what you are left with after you have disentangled your way through the lexical manipulation. This poetry *imposes* a vision on the reader, it points back in on itself. At the bottom of this poetry there is only the poet. This can sometimes work, there is pleasure to be found in it, but the sort of poetry Kenneth White is looking for is one in which you are invited to see with your *own* eyes, and at the bottom of this poetry there is not merely a poet, but *a world opening out*, an original world which embraces the poet, you, everything as part of itself.

Kenneth White's poetry, then, is not a poetry which is wrapped up in metaphors or playing clever games with language but with little to say. Nor a poetry which attempts to pull you into the personal and social concerns of the writer. Rather it is a poetry which 'opens up spaces', offering the reader a way into a perception of the world. It is demanding poetry, but it is accessible poetry – the depths and heights which it penetrates are for the reader to move into. Its rhythms have a natural elemental voice, and the carefully composed music of vowel and consonant sound out the images of water, stone, tree, wind and bird. What we have is an audible, tangible, visual image of the earth which reflects the living movement of the mind, both coming together, earth and mind, in a perception of essential world.

This is not to say that 'form' is irrelevant. It may be correct in some degree to say that White reveals a certain distrust of style[33] (although there is a lot more 'craftsmanship' in White's poetry than is initially apparent), but there is no lack of form. On the contrary, the 'poetics' in 'geopoetics' refers precisely to the idea of 'composition'. The focus of the poet's attention, though, is, primarily, not on (artificial) form, but on that point at which essential perception of the world, so truly felt as to necessitate its being expressed, meets its form in its emergence into being (its voicing).

'No metaphor-mongering/no myth-malarkey', says Ovid in White's 'Ovid's Report'[34], which offers a useful example of White's content and method. 'Ovid's Report' is one of those longer poems of White's which trace the itinerary of an intellectual nomad figure, a type leaving the norms of the social context, in Ovid's case unwillingly through exile, and adventuring out into wider more open spaces of the world. It is this 'exteriorisation' that begins to lead him towards vaster and clearer fields of perception. 'At first I found it hard to swallow,' says the Roman poet of his exile 'on the Scythian coast':

> *the stench of swine and seaweed*
> *offended my delicate nostrils*

Then:

> *the citizenship of Rome*
> *dropped off me*
> *like some old skin*

and he foresees the end of Rome in its already 'polluted, overpopulated' decadence:

One day
thanks to some frozen river
barbarian hordes
will sweep down over the Latin lands
rushing to meet their future

He, though, has 'gone the other way [. . .] up North' and he begins to delight in this 'land of wind and shadow' which is 'at the world's edge'. Normal perception will see 'at the world's edge' as meaning 'the world's end'. In the intellectual nomad's perspective, it means 'the world's beginning'. Now, Ovid contemplates the known world in a map given to him years ago by a Greek sailor, and speculates on unknown worlds beyond the Europe 'we all know (or think we do)':

between the Scythians and the Hyperboreans
a hundred peoples, a thousand tribes
Rome has never heard of:
the Gull Folk
the Star-seekers
the Seal-hunters
the People of the Mist
the Sons of the Wind
the Lonely Ones
the Stone Folk
and so on
ever more and more strange
those who wear shadows
those who fish in emptiness

With such fictitious name lists some of which make obvious references to peoples familiar to us but which are beyond the world as recognised, at least officially, in Ovid's time, White creates an interplay between the voice of the Roman and the inner voice of his reader which opens up the world.

Ovid, through his engagement with his new landscape, begins to discover the 'strange poetry hidden/in these barbarian lands' where the fish are

> *like slivers of a dreamworld*
> *meditations in the flesh*

The poem finishes with Ovid seeking to 'get further into the unspoken space' and

> *find, who knows, the source*
> *of another light*

The poem starts in apparently prosaic form, its tone bitter and proud – 'just imagine me [. . .] all alone among uncouth clods' – with Ovid still writing his 'finely wrought discourses'. But as the rough, cold, Black Sea landscape begins to penetrate, images of it begin to accumulate in the conversational tone, signs of an enlargening and illuminating perspective growing in the Latin poet. In a river-like movement common to many of these poems, the poem's rhythm, mirroring its content, becomes slower and more open, growing calmer as it grows more aware of the expansive void to which the content has directed itself: the geopoetical sea of potentiality opening up at the end which is, in fact, a beginning.

A number of White's longer poems are like 'Ovid's Report'. We can compare Ovid's determination to find both a 'new roughness' and a 'new clearness' in his linguistic expression with Brandan's, in 'Brandan's Last Voyage'[35]:

> *well, it wasn't polish and finesse he wanted*
> *it was a freshness and a force*
> *and a beauty that they'd never know!*

or with the voice of 'Labrador'[36] which talks of

> *a poetry*
> *as unobtrusive as breathing*
> *a poetry like the wind*
> *and the maple leaf*

These and similar poems share the picture of the intellectual nomad, sometimes as in 'Finisterra', for example, or 'Scotia Deserta' this figure being White himself directly, turning aside from the socio-personal context towards a 'sense of world', finding the need to express that sense and the need to find a new type of language and form for that expression, an expression of which he says in 'Broken Ode to White Brittany'[37]:

> *may it never, don't forget*
> *smell the poet.*

Other longer poems describe a natural situation or an intense meditative experience in the landscape such as 'Cape Breton Uplight'[38] or 'The Region of Identity'[39] or 'Interpretations of a Twisted Pine'[40] or 'Crow Meditation Text'[41]. Often the search for true perception, live contact with the world, is saved from over-earnestness by a sense of humour which pervades White's work and which again can lead sometimes to the charge of flippancy, to the feeling that what he is writing is 'light'. Once more this misses the point. The humour is very much part of the oral nature of the writing: it stresses the ordinariness of the experiences being recounted without undermining the sense of difficulty in the process of heading towards enlightenment; it reinforces the idea that perception of reality need not be a matter of transcendentalism, of great religious or philosophical systematising, rather it is a question of 'seeing with (the) eyes' of those who live in intimate contact with the earth like the old man in 'Achawakamik'[42].

There is, then, a great deal of the oral in White's writing, another element which puts some critics off as they feel it to be patronising or indeed simply non-poetic. But the move to see the extraordinary in the ordinary and to say it in an 'ordinary way' is part integral of White's poetics. Taoist and Zen texts do it all the time. As for the frequent listing of books and names, which can be irritating for some, this type of writing is also not without precedent if one remembers the listing of names and places in the tradition of Gaelic poetry.

These are some of the key elements of White's long poems.

In the short poem form, a sense of apparent prosaicness similar to the one evoked above can be evidenced, as in this image of Venice:

HOTEL WINDOW, EVENING

Night falling
voices fading from the quays

gondoliers covering their barques

and suddenly, all along the lagoon
the lighting up of the hidden channels.[43]

The ordinary scene from the window reveals illuminating signs of a hidden reality, the light which the darkness reveals to those who can see it. And the poet must say, as well as see it, in a language apparently as ordinary as the scene but also full of signs brought to the reader's attention by slight rhymes, alliteration and word echoes which, in unifying the poem as a complete image, offer the reader the opportunity to see exactly what the poet has seen, again unifying the reader's mind with the poet's.

The following short poems exemplify this. Each of them, like so many others, gives me (when I am open to them as they are open to me) that shiver that you experience when in the presence of an authentically evoked perception. 'Ludaig Jetty'[44] begins with an image of the social day-to-day world which, as the school-bus leaves, is disrobed like a skin, leaving a naked image of the earth evoked in the light, rock and water of the landscape. I'd point particularly to the use of colour, as in the poem we looked at earlier, 'Morning Walk'[45]. This apt placing of colour is one of the characteristics of White's poetry – he seems to know exactly when and where to place his colours for maximum effect. I'd like also to draw attention to the 'lip-lip-lipping' which does not simply evoke a sound, but is one of those earth-erotic images which are also astutely placed throughout White's writing, like the 'moist, mouldering leaves' of 'Morning Walk':

LUDAIG JETTY

The small motorboat has puttered its way
out to the fishing
the bus has passed by
to collect the children for school
the red postal van
has delivered the mail

now here at Ludaig jetty
there is only
the wind and the light
the cry of a peewit
and the lip-lip-lipping
of grey water on white sand.

'On the Quay at Lannion'[46] has a similar effect but it is difficult to explain why. It has something to do with the last two lines and the way they emerge from the colloquial tone of the preceding lines. There is a primeval quality about them, the *hollow rocks* having a similar effect as *ancient pond* in Basho's famous haiku, an effect which transforms the woman's colloquial *our place* into a kind of mythical statement – the 'our' does not only apply to the women nor only to their community, but also to the poet and then to all of us:

ON THE QUAY AT LANNION

There they were
on the quay at Lannion
mother and daughter
selling spider-crabs

> *big ones, real beauts*
> *and I said*
> *where were those fished from*
> *our place, she said*
>
> *Paimpol*
> *beyond the hollow rocks.*

Metaphor is absent from White's writing unless we see the whole poem or prose narrative as metaphor (what carries you over) in the original sense of the Greek word highlighted humorously by White in this short poem:

> *Standing at the stasis*
> *waiting for the metaphor:*
> *night ride Delfi-Athina.*[47]

the word 'metaphor' in modern Greek meaning a 'bus'. However, other conventional poetic techniques are very evident. Vowels are used to suggest opening and to slow down the rhythm of the writing in the interests of opening up the 'sense of world'. Similarly, consonants are used to evoke ideas of animals, birds, water, trees and wind in ways which are often so discreet as to be barely noticeable. What White is exploiting, suitably for his purpose, is often the inherent onomatopoeia in words, the original root of words in the sound and touch of the things of the earth which they name. This movement from description of the things of the world to an opening out into a general 'sense of world' mirrored in the formal movement from consonant emphasis to vowel can be seen in this beautiful little example of White's 'erotic logic', 'Of the Way South'[48]:

> *Among the dark sand*
> *and the rosy seaweed*
>
> *the deep-curved*
> *sea-white clam shell*
>
> *she is scattered*
> *over all the earth.*

Similarly, Brandan[49] lists the names of the places he passes through, names full of that rich consonant mix of Gaelic and Norse to be found in the Hebrides:

> *Skerryvore and Barra Head*
> *Loch Alsh and Kyle Rhea*

praises these 'clear sounding words' and senses through them

> *a world*
> *opening, opening.*

Again we can note the erotic suggestion in those lines, present also in the closing words of 'In the Nashvak Night'[50] where a quiet world of a lake upon which birds are asleep is awoken in the morning when

> *dawn comes*
> *with the cry of the wild goose.*

In 'Brandan's Last Voyage' the straight use of onomatopoeia to evoke the sounds of birds is done in such a way as to suggest that these sounds of the world have significance:

> *Ka! kaya gaya! keeya! keeya!*
> *branta branta! branta branta!*
> *graak! graak! graak!*

In the first line, the first three words, apparently just sound effects, evoke Egyptian *ka* (energy), Sanskrit *kaya* (body) and Provençal *gaya* (as in Gaya Scienza), while the *keeya* suggests an interrogative (French *'qui est là?'* – 'who's there? who's there?'). The second line might evoke a nominal ('Brandan'), and the third, perhaps constitute a kind of greeting.

In other poems the consonantal emphasis can suggest the socio-political world while the vowel emphasis evokes the natural, as in this from 'The Armorican Manuscript'[51]:

> *pelagian space*
> *what was left out and behind*
> *when the roads were built*
> *and the codes of command*
> *crammed into the mind*
> *what was left out*
> *becoming more and more*
> *faintly articulate*
>
> *still there in the gull cry*
> *the wave clash*
> *those darknesses, those lights*
> *(but who hears? who sees?*
> *who can say?)*

Gerard Manley Hopkins, drawing on Duns Scotus' *haecceitas*, sought to express phenomenal reality and to forge the language which it necessitated. T. S. Eliot exposed the 'wasteland' of Western culture to the critical analysis of the poetic imagination. Ezra Pound, influenced by Fenollosa, re-oriented Western poetry towards the 'image', which would, when perfected, become the building block for long, all-embracing poems. Hugh MacDiarmid pointed to the knowledge of all the disciplines of human endeavour and knowledge as the true subject-matter of poetry. Kenneth White has taken up these most significant attempts to return poetry to its central role as clear and perceptive expression of human experience in the world and renewer of culture. But more than that, he has developed them, and evolved a poetic language which is as remarkable for its simplicity, its musicality and its oral tone as it is for its intensity, profundity and formal astuteness.

The 'possibilism' which he espouses does not see 'endgame' in the degeneration of Western culture, but new beginnings:

> Today, for the first time in the history of humanity, winds blow from all regions of the globe at once, and each and everyone of us has access to all the cultures of the world. That can give rise to cacophony, to disarray, lassitude in front of so much accumulated richness, but it can also give rise, with analytical work and synthesis . . . to a new way of thinking, a great world poem, liveable by everyone.[52]

NOTES

1. The edition White used, bought second-hand for six shillings when he was fifteen (it is still in his library) was the one put out by Chatto & Windus, London, in 1900.

2. This phrase and the following are from White in conversation with the author.

3. In *Le Monde ouvert de Kenneth White*.

4. Book II, 'De la praesumption'. I quote White's translation.

5. *Pilgrim of the Void*, p. 129.

6. *Ibid.*, p. 21.

7. *Ibid.*, p. 215.

8. *The Blue Road*, p. 46.

9. *Ibid.*, p. 41.

10. *Les Limbes incandescents*, p. 43. Quoted from the original English manuscript.

11. *Ibid.*, p. 33.

12. And maybe, fleetingly, in a Joyceian kind of way, '*Sein*', as in Heidegger's *Sein und Zeit* ('Being and Time').

13. *Letters from Gourgounel*, p. 185.

14. *The Blue Road*, p. 93.

15. White knows Gibbon's work well, and is interested. But he does not accept his Golden Age theory, and finds his linguistic method in the *Quair* overdone.

16. *Hokusaï, ou l'horizon sensible*, p. 12.

17. *Pilgrim of the Void*, p. 176.

18. In *The Poetics of Space*, trans. Maria Jolas, Boston, Beacon Press, 1969.

19. *Travels in the Drifting Dawn*, p. 247.

20. *Pilgrim of the Void*, p. 247.

21. The lecture was entitled 'Le long de la route bleue' ('Along the Blue Road'). With additions, it appears in *L'Esprit nomade*, as 'Le projet postmoderne'. Taken up again in *The Wanderer and his Charts* as 'Writing the Road'.

22. *Hokusaï*, p. 96.

23. The essay is entitled 'La musique du monde'.

24. I refer back to the second chapter of Part Two, and the evocation of the chapter 'Sounds' in *Walden*.

25. 'Late August on the Coast', in *The Bird Path*, p. 230–239. *Open World*, p. 588–597.

26. *Scotland's Music*, Edinburgh, Mainstream Publishing, 1992.

27. This is from a limited edition book by White with the photographer Patrick Le Bescont: *Murmures du paysage*, Filigranes, 1991. Translation by Tony McManus. The text is taken up again, integrated into a larger whole, in the chapter 'The Paths of Stone and Wind' of *House of Tides*.

28. *Une apocalypse tranquille*, not yet available in English.

29. *Le Plateau de l'albatros*, not yet available in English. This book of 360 pages makes an approach to geopoetics from the scientific, philosophical and poetic points of

view, bringing in examples from Humboldt, Thoreau and many others.

30. White has used this summary definition of geopoetics in several lectures.

31. Bachelard, *The Poetics of Space*.

32. 'In the Sea and Pine Country', *The Bird Path*, p. 102–106. *Open World*, p. 294–297.

33. Like Artaud (see White's book *Le Monde d'Antonin Artaud*), who was exasperated whenever, engaged in writing, he saw himself 'getting stylish', and resorted to cries or glossological invention. Céline, for his part, also referred to by White in this context, talked of *constipation styliforme*.

34. 'Ovid's Report', *The Bird Path*, p. 34–40. *Open World*, p. 509–514.

35. 'Brandan's Last Voyage', *The Bird Path*, p. 188–193. *Open World*, p. 515–519.

36. 'Labrador', *The Bird Path*, p. 181–185. *Open World*, p. 520–525.

37. 'Broken Ode to White Brittany', *The Bird Path*, p. 205–209. *Open World*, p. 501–504.

38. 'Cape Breton Uplight', *The Bird Path*, p. 93–97. *Open World*, p. 217–220.

39. 'The Region of Identity', *The Bird Path*, p. 97–100. *Open World*, p. 202–204.

40. 'Interpretations of a Twisted Pine', *The Bird Path*, p. 79–81. *Open World*, p. 213–214.

41. 'Crow Meditation Text', *The Bird Path*, p. 106–109. *Open World*, p. 279–282.

42. 'Achawakamik', *Handbook for the Diamond Country*, p. 142. *Open World*, p. 404.

43. This is part of a sequence entitled 'Venetian Notes', in the bilingual *Les Rives du silence*, p. 190–197. *Open World*, p. 461–464.

44. 'Ludaig Jetty', *Handbook for the Diamond Country*, p. 75. *Open World*, p. 119.

45. 'Morning Walk', *Handbook for the Diamond Country*, p. 17. *Open World*, p. 58.

46. 'On the Quay at Lannion', *Handbook for the Diamond Country*, p. 184. *Open World*, p. 440.

47. Again, part of a sequence, 'Five Little Greek Ones', *Handbook for the Diamond Country*, p. 106. *Open World*, p. 370.

48. Part of the sequence 'The Bird Path', in *The Bird Path*, p. 76–79. *Open World*, p. 208–210.

49. 'Brandan's Last Voyage', *The Bird Path*, p. 188–193. *Open World*, p. 515–519.

50. 'In the Nashvak Night', *The Bird Path*, p. 186–187. *Open World*, p. 567–568.

51. 'The Armorican Manuscript', *The Bird Path*, p. 209–211. *Open World*, p. 493–500.

52. Kenneth White, 'L'aventure poétique', in the review *Sources*, vol. 32, Namur, 1991, p. 44. Translated by Kenneth White for Tony McManus.

Kenneth White
English Bibliography

Poetry

Wild Coal, Paris, Club des Étudiants d'anglais de la Sorbonne, 1963.

The Cold Wind of Dawn, London, Jonathan Cape, 1966.

The Most Difficult Area, London, Cape Goliard, 1968.

The Bird Path, collected longer poems, Edinburgh and London, Mainstream Publishing, 1989.

Handbook for the Diamond Country, collected shorter poems, Edinburgh and London, Mainstream Publishing, 1990.

Open World, Collected Poems 1960–2000, Edinburgh, Polygon, 2003.

Narrative

Letters from Gourgounel, London, Jonathan Cape, 1966.

Travels in the Drifting Dawn, Edinburgh and London, Mainstream Publishing, 1989.

The Blue Road, Edinburgh and London, Mainstream Publishing, 1990.

Pilgrim of the Void, Edinburgh and London, Mainstream Publishing, 1992.

House of Tides, Edinburgh, Polygon, 2000.

Across the Territories, Edinburgh, Polygon, 2004.

Essays

The Coast Opposite Humanity, an essay on the poetry of Robinson Jeffers, Carmarthen, Unicorn Bookshop, 1975.

The Tribal Dharma, an essay on the work of Gary Snyder, Carmarthen, Unicorn Bookshop, 1975.

The Life-technique of John Cowper Powys, Swansea, Galloping Dog Press, 1978.

Van Gogh and Kenneth White, An Encounter, Paris, Flohic Éditions, 1994.

On Scottish Ground, Edinburgh, Polygon, 1998.

Geopoetics: Place, Culture, World, Glasgow, Alba Editions, 2003.

The Wanderer and his Charts, Edinburgh, Polygon, 2004.

On the Atlantic Edge, Dingwall, Sandstone Press, 2006.

Interviews

Coast to Coast, Glasgow, Open World Editions and Mythic Horse Press, 1996.

Translations

Showing the Way, a Hmong Initiation of the Dead, Bangkok, Pandora, 1983.

André Breton, *Selected Poems*, London, Jonathan Cape, 1969.

André BRETON, *Ode to Charles Fourier*, London, Cape Goliard Press, 1969.

Recorded poetry

Into the White World, Essays on the Work of Kenneth White, two cassettes of poem readings, Scotsoun, 13 Ashton Rd, Glasgow G12 8SP, 1992.

On Kenneth White's work

Gavin BOWD, Charles FORSDICK and Norman BISSELL (eds), *Grounding a World*, essays by various authors, St Andrews University Symposium, Glasgow, Alba Editions, 2005.

French Bibliography

Poésie

En toute candeur, éd. bilingue, trad. Pierre Leyris, Paris, Mercure de France, 1964.

Mahamudra, le grand geste, éd. bilingue, trad. Marie-Claude White, Paris, Mercure de France, 1979.

Le Grand Rivage, éd. bilingue, trad. Patrick Guyon et Marie-Claude White, Paris, Le Nouveau Commerce, 1980.

Scènes d'un monde flottant, éd. bilingue revue et augmentée, trad. Marie-Claude White, Paris, Grasset, 1983.

Terre de diamant, éd. bilingue revue et augmentée, trad. Philippe Jaworski, Marie-Claude White, Paris, Grasset, 1983. Nouvelle édition, Paris, Grasset, Les Cahiers rouges, 2003.

Atlantica, éd. bilingue, trad. Marie-Claude White, Paris, Grasset, 1986. Prix Alfred de Vigny.

Les Rives du silence, éd. bilingue, trad. Marie-Claude White, Paris, Mercure de France, 1997.

Limites et Marges, éd. bilingue, trad. Marie-Claude White, Paris, Mercure de France, 2000.

Le Passage extérieur, éd. bilingue, trad. Marie-Claude White, Paris, Mercure de France, 2005.

Récits

Les Limbes incandescents, trad. Patrick Mayoux, Paris, Denoël, Les Lettres nouvelles, 1976. Nouvelle édition, Paris, Denoël, 1990.

Dérives, plusieurs traducteurs, Paris, Laffont, Lettres Nouvelles /Maurice Nadeau, 1978.

Lettres de Gourgounel, trad. Gil et Marie Jouanard, Paris, Presses d'aujourd'hui, 1979. Nouvelle édition, Paris, Grasset, Les Cahiers rouges, 1986.

L'Écosse avec Kenneth White, Paris, Flammarion, 1980. Réédition Arthaud, 1988.

Le Visage du vent d'est, trad. Marie-Claude White, Paris, Les

Presses d'aujourd'hui, 1980.

La Route bleue, trad. Marie-Claude White, Paris, Grasset, 1983. Prix Médicis étranger. Livre de poche n° 5988.

Les Cygnes sauvages, trad. Marie-Claude White, Paris, Grasset, 1990.

Corsica, l'itinéraire des rives et des monts, trad. Marie-Claude White, Ajaccio, La Marge, 1999.

La Maison des marées, trad. Marie-Claude White, Paris, Albin Michel, 2005.

Le Rôdeur des confins, trad. Marie-Claude White, Paris, Albin Michel, 2006.

Essais

La Figure du dehors, Paris, Grasset, 1982. Livre de poche, Biblio essais 4105.

Une apocalypse tranquille, Paris, Grasset, 1985.

L'Esprit nomade, Paris, Grasset, 1987.

Le Monde d'Antonin Artaud, Bruxelles et Paris, Éditions Complexe, 1989.

Hokusaï ou l'horizon sensible, Paris, Terrain Vague, 1990.

Le Plateau de l'albatros, introduction à la géopoétique, Paris, Grasset, 1994.

Les Finisterres de l'esprit, Cléguer, Éditions du Scorff, 1998.

Une stratégie paradoxale, essais de résistance culturelle, Bordeaux, Presses Universitaires de Bordeaux, 1998.

Entretiens

Le Poète cosmographe, Bordeaux, Presses Universitaires de Bordeaux, 1987.

Le Lieu et la parole, 1987–1997, Cléguer, Éditions du Scorff, 1997.

Le Champ du grand travail, Bruxelles, Didier Devillez Éditeur, 2002.

L'Ermitage des brumes, Paris, Dervy, 2005.

Sur l'œuvre de Kenneth White

Michèle DUCLOS (dir.), *Le Monde ouvert de Kenneth White*, essais et témoignages par divers auteurs, Bordeaux, Presses Universitaires de Bordeaux, 1995.

Jean-Jacques WUNENBURGER (dir.), *Autour de Kenneth White: espace, pensée poétique*, essais par divers auteurs, Dijon, Presses Universitaires de Dijon, 1996.

Olivier DELBARD, *Les lieux de Kenneth White, paysage, pensée, poétique*, Paris, L'Harmattan, 1999.

Pierre JAMET, *Le local et le global dans l'œuvre de Kenneth White*, Paris, L'Harmattan, 2002.

Jean-Yves KERGUELEN, *Kenneth White et la Bretagne*, Moëlan-sur-Mer, Éditions Blanc Silex, 2002.

Michèle DUCLOS, *Kenneth White: Nomade intellectuel, poète du monde*, Grenoble, ELLUG – Université Stendhal, 2006.

Laurent MARGANTIN (dir.), *Kenneth White et la Géopoétique*, Paris, L'Harmattan, 2006.